George Thomas Rider

Lyra Anglicana

Or, A Hymnal of sacred Poetry

George Thomas Rider

Lyra Anglicana
Or, A Hymnal of sacred Poetry

ISBN/EAN: 9783337076962

Printed in Europe, USA, Canada, Australia, Japan

Cover: Foto ©ninafisch / pixelio.de

More available books at **www.hansebooks.com**

Lyra Anglicana

OR A Hymnal of Sacred Poetry

Selected from the best English Writers

AND ARRANGED AFTER THE ORDER OF THE

APOSTLE'S CREED

BY THE

Rev. GEORGE T. RIDER, M.A.

"O YE SERVANTS OF THE LORD ... PRAISE HIM HIM FOREVER & MAGNIFY ... BLESS YE THE LORD"

NEW YORK
D. APPLETON & CO.
1865.

Lyra Anglicana;

OR,

A HYMNAL OF SACRED POETRY.

SELECTED FROM THE BEST

ENGLISH WRITERS,

AND ARRANGED AFTER THE ORDER OF THE

APOSTLES' CREED.

BY THE

REV. GEORGE T. RIDER, M.A.

NEW YORK:
D. APPLETON & COMPANY,
443 and 445 Broadway.
1865.

ENTERED, according to Act of Congress, in the year 1864, by
D. APPLETON AND COMPANY,
In the Clerk's Office of the District Court of the United States for the Southern District of New York.

PREFACE.

The Lyric, rather than the Polemic spirit, is the fairer witness of a living Christianity. Periods of scholastic heat are periods of ethical chill. When the Church goes forth in her militant greatness, overthrowing strongholds of darkness and death, she is garlanded with hymns and spiritual songs. Flushed with springtime fulness of the Indwelling Presence, her heart wakes into Praise and Thanksgiving.

In her conquering march she keeps step to the rhythm and cadence of her stirring chant and hymn.

Ambrose, Luther, and the Wesleys wrought to such music; and perhaps their Hymns are stronger and more persuasive with us, than are their Definitions of Faith and Doctrine.

Hence, while the Ages all the way down, are littered with stranded controversies, wasted and wasting, the dead leaves and blasted fruit of aimless thinking; their Hymns live with us, quick with spiritual forces, unspent and yet warm with the great love that inspired them.

We reject their Definitions, and accept their Hymns, finding the Fellowship of Praise wholesome, and large enough for all our wants, overliving and outliving all that is merely incidental and extrinsic to the Church **Life.**

Hymns are personal disclosures of the inner life: they bring to us all that is communicable of "the fruits of the Spirit." They come to us with all that words are permitted to bear of ecstacy, the trance and the vision. They are, then, our **sweetest** sureties of the greatness and reality of the regenerate life,—of its promise and prophecy.

The Hymnology of English Christianity, representing so many widely-remote cultures, interpenetrated with such rapturous, forceful impulses, prismatic with such variously-hued yet blended experiences, stands eminently alone and unequalled in its wealth and beauty.

At the outset, kindled by the **calm fervor of** the Missal and Breviary Hymns, and the glowing symbolism of a Church still guarding the fires of the early faith, the Lyric spirit is felt among the first developments of our Language, while the Anglican Church was emerging from the bondage of a dead tongue and dead superstitions. And recalling the general and cordial reception of the Christian Faith throughout England, we find full explanation of the Christian temper more or less clearly defined in nearly all her poetry.

Thus the Church at the Reformation found a new language waiting to do its bidding: a language that had grown with her own growth, and developed an energy and wealth of resource, while yet in its infancy, equal to the illustrious service of her Evangelists or Psalmists:—the language of Spenser and Shakespeare, George Withers and Herbert, of Hooker and Barrow, of Newton and Bacon.

The present posture of English Christianity is a complex result of many vital movements, at different times, acting from different centres of power. They have each and all wrought for the shaping of the structure as it now stands.

This compilation undertakes to register something of the Lyric spirit of this varied history; and not without some reference to the proportions and relations which seem to have obtained between the Ecclesiastic and Subjective, the Retrospective and Prophetic tendencies which in their turn have quickened the Church.

During the preparation of this work nothing has been more clearly manifest, than the continual recurrence of deep and earnest *unisons of feeling—unisons of experimental life and Christian consciousness*, especially touching the Adorable Person and Offices of our Lord, floating down from age to age, in such unfailing sweetness, that a Christianity, which, to the Theologian, lies the fragment of a perished Unity, finds its way to the heart of the Worshipper clothed upon with the freshness of a living, loving Presence, among the Faithful, ministering in the name and stead of its Lord.

The Poetry selected, is not generally found in American reprints; and a large part, it is believed, reaches the general reader for the first time in this volume.

G. T. R.

Index of Subjects.

ARRANGED ACCORDING TO THE APOSTLES' CREED.

                                              PAGES

FAITH.
    I believe . . . . . 1—8

GOD AND PROVIDENCE.
    In God the Father Almighty, maker of Heaven and Earth, . . 9—30

THE INCARNATION.
    And in Jesus Christ His only Son our Lord; Who was conceived by the Holy Ghost, Born of the Virgin Mary, . . . 31—64

THE ATONEMENT.
    Suffered under Pontius Pilate, was crucified, dead, and buried; He descended into Hell, ... 65—108

THE RESURRECTION.
    The third day He rose from the dead; . 109—124

PAGES

THE ASCENSION.

    He ascended into Heaven, And sitteth on the right hand of God the Father Almighty; . . . 125—149

SECOND COMING AND JUDGMENT.

    From thence he shall come to judge the quick and the dead. . . . 150—172

THE HOLY SPIRIT.

    I believe in the Holy Ghost, . . 173—184

FELLOWSHIP OF CHRIST.

    The Holy Catholic Church,
    The Communion of Saints, . . 185—214
    The Forgiveness of sins, . . . 215—229

TIME AND ETERNITY.

    The Resurrection of the body, And The Life everlasting. Amen. . . 229—288

Index of First Lines.

	PAGE
Abide with me; fast falls the eventide	244
And am I here, and my Redeemer gone?	100
A pathway opens from the tomb	111
At length the worst is o'er, and Thou art laid	102
A thousand years have fleeted	194
At the cross, her station keeping	79
Awake glad heart! get up and sing	31
Away with sorrow's sigh	33
Behold the Lamb!	83
Beneath my cross I lay me down	85
Blessed Creatour! let Thine only Sonne	9
Brief life is here our portion	268
But how shall we be glad?	228
By Christ redeemed, in Christ restored	156
Come lovely name! life of our hope	50

Index of First Lines.

	PAGE
Come to our poor nature's night	173
Come wandering sheep, O come!	197
Day of anger, that dread Day	162
Dear saviour of a dying world	117
Emmanuel, Thy name we sing	40
Far from the Shepherd's one true fold I stray	259
False world, thou ly'st: thou canst not lend	282
For thee, O dear, dear Country	269
Go worship at Immanuel's feet	138
Hark! hark! my soul! angelic songs are swelling	277
Head of the Hosts in glory!	136
He cometh on yon hallowed Board	207
Here I sink before Thee lowly	210
His mother cannot reach His face	77
Holy Spirit, gently come	183
Holy Spirit given	175
Holy Spirit, Lord of Light	177
Hosanna to the living Lord!	154
How brightly dawns the Morning Star	59
I journey through a desert drear and wild	171
I love, and have some cause to love the earth	10
I made a posy while the day ran by	273

Index of First Lines.

	PAGE
In token that thou shalt not fear	203
I say to thee, do thou repent	190
Is it not strange the darkest hour	93
I worship Thee, sweet Will of God!	7
Jerusalem the golden!	271
Jesu is in my heart; His sacred name	82
Jesus mighty sufferer! say	71
Jesu! the very thought of Thee	144
Joy of my life while left me here!	128
Just as I am—without one plea	252
Lead, kindly light, amid the encircling gloom	6
Let me be with Thee where Thou art	221
Let the storms ply their deep and threatening bass	192
Little pomp of earthly state	61
Lo! He comes with clouds descending	168
Long did I toil and knew no earthly rest	198
Lord! come away!	158
Lord God of might, in reverence lowly	134
Lord, many times I am aweary quite	55
Lord what a change within us one short hour	215
My God and Father, while I stray	17
My Lord, my Love was crucified	96
My Saviour can it ever be	130
Not here! not here! where the sparkling waters	275
Not Thou from us, O Lord, but we	251

Index of First Lines.

	PAGE
When God of old came down from Heaven	165
When Jesus came to earth of old	150
When wounded sore, the stricken soul	91
Whilst the **careless** world is sleeping,	152
Who says the wan autumnal sun	113
Who to the golden Sunnes long restless race	19
Why comes this fragrance on the summer breeze?	18
Why dost thou beat so quick, my heart?	4

LORD! I BELIEVE.

GIFT of Gifts! O Grace of Faith!
   My God! how can it be
That Thou, who hast discerning love,
   Shouldst give that gift to me?

How many hearts thou mightst have had
   More innocent than mine!
How many souls more worthy far
   Of that sweet touch of Thine!

Ah, Grace! into unlikeliest hearts
   It is thy boast to come,
The glory of thy light to find
   In darkest spots a home.

How will they die, how will they die,
   How bear the cross of grief,
Who have not got the light of faith,
   The courage of belief?

The crowd of cares, the weightiest cross,
   Seem trifles less than light,—
Earth looks so little and so low
   When faith shines full and bright.

O happy, happy that I am!
   If thou canst be, O Faith!
The treasure that thou art in life,
   What wilt thou be in death?

Thy choice, O God of Goodness! then
   I lovingly adore;
O give me grace to keep thy grace,
   And grace to merit more!

                                FABER.

THE PEACE OF GOD.

THE child leans on its parent's breast,
Leaves there its cares, and is at rest;
The bird sits singing by his nest,
   And tells aloud
His trust in God, and so is blest
    'Neath every cloud.

He has no store, he sows no seed;
Yet sings aloud, and doth not heed;
By flowing stream or grassy mead,
   He sings to shame
Men, who forget, in fear of need,
    A Father's name.

The heart that trusts for ever sings,
And feels as light as it had wings;
A well of peace within it springs:
   Come good, or ill,
Whate'er to-day, to-morrow brings,
    It is His will!
   Isaac Williams, (1842.)

THE FRUIT OF THE SPIRIT IS LOVE, JOY, PEACE.

WHY dost thou beat so quick, my heart?
   Why struggle in thy cage?
What shall I do for thee, poor heart!
   Thy throbbing heat to swage?

What spell is this comes over thee?
   My soul! what sweet surprise?
And wherefore these unbidden tears
   That start into mine eyes?

Thy sweetness hath betrayed Thee, Lord!
   Dear Spirit it is Thou;
Deeper and deeper in my heart
   I feel thee nestling now.

Thy home is with the simple, Lord!
   The simple are thy rest;
Thy lodging is in child-like hearts;
   Thou makest there Thy nest.

Dear Comforter! Eternal Love!
  If Thou wilt stay with me,
Of lowly thoughts and simple ways
  I'll build a nest for Thee.

My heart, sweet Dove! I'll lend to Thee
  To mourn with at Thy will;
My tongue shall be Thy lute to try
  On sinners' souls Thy skill.

Who made this beating heart of mine,
  But Thou my heavenly Guest?
Let no one have it then but Thee,
  And let it be Thy nest.

FABER.

THE TRUE LIGHT.

LORD, kindly Light, amid the encircling
   gloom,
  Lead Thou me on!
The night is dark and I am far from
   home;
  Lead Thou me on!
Keep Thou my feet; I do not ask to see
The distant way; one step's enough for me.

I was not ever thus, nor prayed that Thou
   Wouldst lead me on;
I loved to see and choose my path, but now
   Lead Thou me on!
I loved the garish day, and, spite of fears,
Pride ruled my will: remember not past years.

So long Thy power hath kept me, sure it still
   Will lead me on!
O'er moor and fen, o'er crag and torrent, till
   The night is gone,
And with the morn those angel faces smile
Which I have loved long since and lost awhile.
        NEWMAN.

NOT AS I WILL, BUT AS THOU WILT.

I WORSHIP thee, sweet Will of God!
   And all thy ways adore,
And every day I live I seem
   To love thee more and more.

Thou wert the end, the blessed rule
   Of Jesus' toils and tears;
Thou wert the passion of His Heart
   Those Three-and-Thirty years.

I love to kiss each print where thou
   Hast set thine unseen feet:
I cannot fear the blessed Will!
   Thine empire is so sweet.

When obstacles and trials seem
   Like prison-walls to be,
I do the little that I can do,
   And leave the rest to thee.

I have no cares, O blessed Will!
　For all my cares are thine;
I live in triumph, Lord! for Thou
　Hast made Thy triumphs mine.

Ride on, ride on triumphantly,
　Thou glorious Will! ride on;
Faith's pilgrim sons behind thee take
　The road that thou hast gone.

He always wins who rides with God,
　To him no chance is lost;
God's will is sweetest to him when
　It triumphs at his cost.

Ill that He blesses is our good,
　And noblest good is ill;
And all is right that seems most wrong,
　If it be his sweet Will!

FABER.

HE THAT HATH THE SON, HATH LIFE.

BLESSED Creatour! let thine only Sonne,
 Sweete blossome, stock and roote of David's line
 The cleare, bright Morning-Starre give light and shine
On my poor spirit; which hath new-begunne
With his love's praise, and with vaine loves hath donne.
 To my poor muse let him his ears incline
 Thirsting to taste of that celestial wine
Whose purple streams hath our salvation wonne.
 O gracious Bridegroom! and thrice lovely Bride!
Which—'Come and fill who will'—forever crie:
 'Water of life to no man is deny'de;
'Fill still who will—if any man be drie,'
O heavenly voice! I thirst, I thirst, and come
For life with other sinners to get some.

BARNABAS BARNES, (1596.)

DELIGHT IN GOD ONLY.

I LOVE (and have some cause to love) the earth;
   She is my Maker's creature; therefore good:
She is my mother, for she gave me birth;
   She is my tender nurse—she gives me food;
But what's a creature, Lord, compared with Thee?
Or what's my mother, or my nurse to me?

I love the air: her dainty sweets refresh
   My drooping soul, and to new sweets invite me;
Her shrill-mouthed quire sustains me with their flesh,
   And with their polyphonian notes delight me:
But what's the air or all the sweets that she
Can bless my soul withal, compared to Thee?

I love the sea: she is my fellow creature,
   My careful purveyor; she provides me store:
She walls me round; she makes my diet greater;
   She wafts my treasure from a foreign shore:
But Lord of Oceans, when compared with Thee,
What is the ocean or her wealth to me?

To Heaven's high city I direct my journey,
   Whose spangled suburbs entertain mine eye:
Mine eye, by contemplation's great attorney,
   Transcends the crystal pavement of the sky;
But what is Heaven, great God, to Thee?
Without Thy presence, heaven's no heaven to me.

Without Thy presence earth gives no refection;
   Without Thy presence sea affords no treasure;
Without Thy presence air's a rank infection;
   Without Thy presence heaven itself no pleasure:
If not possess'd, if not enjoy'd in Thee,
What's earth or sea or air or heaven to me?

The highest honours that the world can boast,
   Are subjects far too low for my desires;
The brightest beams of glory are (at most)
   But dying sparkles of Thy living fire.
The loudest flames that earth can kindle, be
But nightly glow-worms, if compared to Thee.

Without Thy presence wealth is bags of cares;
   Wisdom but folly; joy disquiet—sadness:
Friendship is treason, and delights are snares,
   Pleasures but pain, and mirth but pleasing madness.

Without Thee, Lord, things be not what they be,
Nor have they being when compared with Thee.

In having all things, and not Thee, what have I?
  Not having Thee, what have my labours got?
Let me enjoy but Thee, what further crave I?
  And having Thee alone, what have I not?
I wish nor sea nor land; nor would I be
Possessed of Heaven, heaven unpossess'd of Thee.

FRANCIS QUARLES.

THE DISCIPLINE OF FAITH.

"The eyes of them that see shall not be dim, and the ears of them that hear shall hearken." *Isaiah*, xxxii. 3.

OF the bright things in earth and air
   How little can the heart embrace!
Soft shades and gleaming lights are
    there—
   I knew it well but cannot trace.

Mine eye unworthy seems to read
   One page of Nature's beauteous book;
It lies before me, fair outspread—
   I only cast a wishful look.

I cannot paint to memory's eye
   The scene, the glance, I dearest love—
Unchanged themselves, in me they die,
   Or faint, or false, their shadows prove.

In vain, with dull and tuneless ear,
   I linger by soft music's cell,
And in my heart of hearts would hear
   What to her own she deigns to tell.

'Tis misty all, both sight and sound—
  I only know 'tis fair and sweet—
'Tis wandering on enchanted ground
  With dizzy brow and tottering feet.

But patience! there may come a time
  When these dull ears shall hear aright
Strains, that outring Earth's drowsy chime,
  As Heaven outshines the taper's light.

These eyes, that dazzled now and weak,
  At glancing motes in sunshine wink,
Shall see the King's full glory break,
  Nor from the blissful vision shrink:

In fearless love and hope uncloyed
  For ever on that ocean bright
Empowered to gaze; and undestroyed,
  Deeper and deeper plunged in light.

Though scarcely now their laggard glance
  Reach to an arrow's flight, that day
They shall behold, and not in trance,
  The region very far away.

If memory sometimes at our spell
  Refuse to speak, or speak amiss,
We shall not need her where we dwell
  Ever in sight of all our bliss.

Meanwhile, if over sea or sky
   Some tender lights unnoticed fleet,
Or on loved features dawn and die,
   Unread, to us, their lesson sweet;

Yet are there saddening sights around,
   Which Heaven, in mercy, spares us too,
And we see far in holy ground,
   If daily purged our mental view.

The distant landscape draws not nigh
   For all our gazing; but the soul,
That upward looks, may still descry
   Nearer, each day, the brightening goal.

And thou, too curious ear, that fain
   Wouldst thread the maze of Harmony,
Content thee with one simple strain,
   The lowlier, sure, the worthier thee;

Till thou art duly trained, and taught
   The concord sweet of Love divine;
Then, with that inward Music fraught,
   For ever rise, and sing, and shine.

KEBLE.

THY GOD, THY GLORY.

FOUNTAIN of light and living breath,
    Whose mercies never fail nor fade!
Fill us with life that hath no death,
    Fill us with light that hath no shade:
Appoint the remnant of our days,
To see Thy power, and sing Thy praise.

Lord God of gods, before whose throne
    Stand storms and fires! O what shall we
Return to heaven that is our own,
    When all the world belongs to Thee?
We have no offering to impart
But praises and a wounded heart.

Great God, whose kingdom hath no end,
    Into whose secrets none can dive,
Whose mercies none can apprehend,
    Whose justice none can feel—and live!
What our dull hearts cannot aspire
To know,—Lord, teach us to admire!

J. QUARLES.

THY WILL BE DONE!

MY GOD and Father, while I stray
Far from my home, or life's rough way,
O teach me from my heart to say,
    Thy will be done!

Though dark my path, and sad my lot,
Let me be still and murmur not,
Or breathe the prayer divinely taught,
    Thy will be done!

What though in lonely grief I sigh
For friends beloved, no longer nigh,
Submissive still would I reply,
    Thy will be done!

Though thou hast called me to resign
What most I prized, it ne'er was mine,
I have but yielded what was Thine;
    Thy will be done!

Should grief or sickness waste away
My life in premature decay,

My Father! still I strive to say,
    Thy will be done!

Let but my fainting heart be blest,
With Thy sweet Spirit for its guest,
My God, to Thee I leave the rest;
    Thy will be done!

Renew my will from day to day;
Blend it with Thine; and take away
All that now makes it hard to say,
    Thy will be done!

Then, when on earth I breathe no more,
The prayer, oft mixed with tears before,
I'll sing upon a happier shore,
    Thy will be done!

    CHARLOTTE ELLIOTT, (1836.)

CANST THOU BY SEARCHING, FIND OUT GOD?

WHO to the golden sunnes long restless race
   Can limit set? What vessel can comprise
The swelling winds? What cunning can devise
With queint arithmetique, in steadfast place
To number all the starres in heaven's pallâce?
   What cunning artist ever was so wise
   Who, by the starres and planets, could advise
Of all adventures the just course and case?
   Who measured hath the waters of the seas?
Who ever in just balance poysed the ayre?
   As no man ever could the least of these
Performe with humaine labour, strength and care,
   So who shall strive, in volumes to contayne
   God's prayes ineffable, contends in vayne.

BARNABAS BARNES, (1596.)

A NAME WHICH IS ABOVE EVERY NAME.

THE sunne of our soul's light! Thee
    would I call:—
  But for our light Thou didst the
    bright sunne make:
Nor reason that Thy majestie should take
The chiefest epithetes at all.
Our chief directions starre celestiall!
  (But that the starres for our direction's sake
  Thou fixed, and canst at pleasure shake)
I would Thee name, The Rocke Substantiall
  Of our assurance, I would tearme Thy name,
But that all rocks by Thy command were made.
  If King of kings, Thy majestie became,
Monarch of monarchs I would have saide—
  But Thou giv'st kingdoms and makes crownes
    unstable;
  By these I know Thy name—Ineffable!

                BARNABAS BARNES, (1596.)

DE PROFUNDIS.

I.

THE face which, duly as the sun,
Rose up for me with life begun,
To mark all bright hours of the day
With hourly love, is dimmed away,—
And yet my days go on, go on.

II.

The tongue which, like a stream, could run
Smooth music from the roughest stone,
And every morning with " Good day "
Make each day good, is hushed away,—
And yet my days go on, go on.

III.

The heart which, like a staff, was one
For mine to lean and rest upon,
The strongest on the longest day
With steadfast love is caught away,—
And yet my days go on, go on.

IV.

And cold before my summer's done,
And deaf in Nature's general tune,
And fallen too low for special fear,
And here, with hope no longer here,—
While the tears drop, my days go on.

V.

The world goes whispering to its own,
"This anguish pierces to the bone;"
And tender friends go sighing round,
"What love can ever cure this wound?"
My days go on, my days go on.

VI.

The past rolls forward on the sun
And makes all night. O dreams begun,
Not to be ended! Ended bliss,
And life that will not end in this!
My days go on, my days go on.

VII.

Breath freezes on my lips to moan:
As one alone, once not alone,
I sit and knock at Nature's door,
Heart-bare, heart-hungry, very poor,
Whose desolated days go on.

VIII.

I knock and cry,—Undone, undone!
Is there no help, no comfort,—none?
No gleaning in the wide wheat-plains
Where others drive their loaded wains?
My vacant days go on, go on.

IX.

This Nature, though the snows be down,
Thinks kindly of the bird of June:
The little red hip on the tree
Is ripe for such. What is for me,
Whose days so winterly go on?

X.

No bird am I to sing in June,
And dare not seek an equal boon.
Good nests and berries red are Nature's
To give away to better creatures,—
And yet my days go on, go on.

XI.

I ask less kindness to be done,—
Only to loose these pilgrim-shoon,
(Too early worn and grimed) with sweat
Cool deathly touch to these tired feet,
Till days go out, which now go on.

XII.

Only to lift the turf unmown
From off the earth where it has grown,
Some cubit-space, and say, "Behold,
Creep in poor Heart, beneath that fold,
Forgetting how the days go on."

XIII.

What harm could that do? Green anon
The sward would quicken, overshone
By skies as blue; and crickets might
Have leave to chirp there day and night
While my new rest went on, went on.

XIV.

From gracious Nature have I won
Such liberal bounty? may I run
So, lizard-like, within her side,
And there be safe, who now am tried
By days that painfully go on?

XV.

A voice reproves me thereupon,
More sweet than Nature's when the drone
Of bees is sweetest, and more deep
Than when the rivers overleap
The shuddering pines, and thunder on.

XVI.

God's voice, not Nature's. Night and noon
He sits upon the great white throne
And listens for the creature's praise.
What babble we of days and days?
The Day-spring He, whose days go on.

XVII.

He reigns above, He reigns alone;
Systems burn out and leave His throne:
Fair mists of seraphs melt and fall
Around Him, changeless amid all,—
Ancient of Days, whose days go on.

XVIII.

He reigns below, He reigns alone,
And, having life in love foregone
Beneath the crown of sorrow thorns,
He reigns the jealous God. Who mourns
Or rules with Him, while days go on?

XIX.

By anguish which made pale the sun,
I hear Him charge His saints that none
Among His creatures anywhere
Blaspheme against Him with despair,
However darkly days go on.

XX.

Take from my head the thorn-wreath brown!
No mortal grief deserves that crown.
O súpreme Love, chief Misery,
The sharp regalia is for Thee
Whose days eternally go on!

XXI.

For us,—whatever's undergone,
Thou knowest, willest what is done.
Grief may be joy misunderstood;
Only the Good discerns the good.
I trust Thee, while my days go on.

XXII.

Whatever's lost, it first was won:
We will not struggle nor impugn.
Perhaps the cup was broken here,
That Heaven's new wine might show
    more clear.
I praise Thee while my days go on.

XXIII.

I praise Thee while my days go on;
I love Thee while my days go on:
Through dark and dearth, through fire and
    frost,

With emptied arms and treasure lost,
I thank Thee while my days go on.

XXIV.

And having in Thy life-depth thrown
Being and suffering (which are one),
As a child drops his pebble small
Down some deep well, and hears it fall
Smiling—so I. THY DAYS GO ON.

  ELIZABETH BARRETT BROWNING.

GOD IS LOVE.

WHY comes this fragrance on the summer breeze,
    The blended tribute of ten thousand flowers,
To me, a frequent wanderer 'mid the trees
    That form these gay though solitary bowers?
One answer is around, beneath, above;
The echo of the voice, that God is Love!

Why bursts such melody from tree and bush,
    The overflowing of each songster's heart,
So filling mine that it can scarcely hush
    Awhile to listen, but would take its part?
'Tis but one song I hear where'er I rove,
Though countless be the notes, that God is Love!

Why leaps the streamlet down the mountain side,
    Hastening so swiftly to the vale beneath,
To cheer the shepherd's thirsty flock, or glide
    Where the hot sun has left a faded wreath,
Or, rippling, aid the music of the grove?
Its own glad voice replies, that God is Love

In starry heavens at the midnight hour,
  In ever-varying hues at morning's dawn,
In the fair bow athwart the falling shower,
  In forest, river, lake, rock, hill, and lawn,
One truth is written: all conspire to prove,
What grace of old revealed, that God is Love!

Nor less the pulse of health, far glancing eye,
  And heart so moved with beauty, perfume, song,
This spirit, soaring through a gorgeous sky,
  Or diving ocean's coral caves among,
Fleeter than a darting fish or startled dove;
All, all declare the same, that God is Love!

Is it a fallen world on which I gaze?
  Am I as deeply fallen as the rest,
Yet joys partaking, past my utmost praise,
  Instead of wandering forlorn and unblest?
It is as if an unseen spirit strove
To grave upon my heart, that God is Love!

Yet wouldst thou see, my soul, this truth displayed
  In characters which wondering angels read,
And read, adoring; go, imploring aid
  To gaze with faith, behold the Saviour bleed!
Thy God, in human form! O what can prove,
If this suffice thee not, that God is Love.

Cling to His cross; and let thy ceaseless prayer
    Be, that thy grasp may fail not! and, ere long
Thou ascend to that fair Temple, where
    In strains ecstatic an innumerous throng
Of saints and seraphs, round the Throne above,
Proclaim for evermore, that God is Love!
THOMAS DAVIS, (1859.)

CHRIST'S NATIVITY.

AWAKE, glad heart! get up, and sing!
It is the Birth-day of thy King.
    Awake! awake!
    The sun doth shake
Light from his locks, and, all the way
Breathing Perfumes, doth spice the day.

Awake, awake! hark how th' *wood* rings,
Winds whisper, and the busie *Springs*
    A Concert make;
    Awake! awake!
Man is their high-priest, and should rise
To offer up the sacrifice.

I would I were some *Bird*, or star,
Fluttering in woods, or lifted far
    Above this *Inne*
    And Rode of sin!
Then either Star or *Bird* should be
Shining or singing still to thee.

I would I had in my best part
Fit roomes for Thee! or that my heart
    Were so clean as
    Thy manger was!
But I am all filth, and obscene;
Yet, if Thou wilt, Thou canst make me clean.

Sweet *Jesu!* will then; let no more
This leper haunt and soyl thy door!
    Cure him, ease him,
    O release him!
And let once more, by mystic birth,
The Lord of life be born in earth.

HENRY VAUGHN.

JAM DESINANT SUSPIRIA.

AWAY with sorrow's sigh,
Our prayers are heard on high;
And through Heaven's crystal door
On this our earthly floor
Comes meek-eyed Peace to walk with poor mortality.

In dead of night profound,
There breaks a seraph sound
Of never-ending morn;
The Lord of glory born
Within a holy grot on this our sullen ground.

Now with that shepherd crowd
If it might be allowed,
We fain would enter there
With awful hastening fear,
And kiss that cradle chaste in reverend worship bowed.

O sight of strange surprise
That fills our gazing eyes:
A manger coldly strew'd,
And swaddling bands so rude,
A leaning mother poor, and child that helpless lies.

Art Thou, O wondrous sight,
Of lights the very Light;
Who holdest in Thy hand
The sky and sea and land;
Who than the glorious heavens are more exceeding bright?

'Tis so; faith darts before,
And, through the cloud drawn o'er,
She sees the God of all,
Where angels prostrate fall,
Adoring tremble still, and trembling still adore.

No thunders round Thee break;
Yet doth Thy silence speak
From that, Thy Teacher's seat,
To us around Thy feet,
To shun what flesh desires, what flesh abhors to seek.

Within us, Babe divine,
Be born, and make us Thine;
Within our souls reveal
Thy love and power to heal;
Be born, and make our hearts Thy cradle and Thy shrine.

ISAAC WILLIAMS, (1839.)

THE NATIVITY.

"And suddenly there was with the Angel a multitude of the heavenly host praising God."

WHAT sudden blaze of song
    Spreads o'er the expanse of
        Heaven?
    In waves of light it thrills along,
    Th' angelic signal given:
"Glory to God!" from yonder central fire
Flows out the echoing lay beyond the starry
    quire;

    Like circles widening round
      Upon a clear blue river,
    Orb after orb, the wondrous sound
      Is echoed on forever:
"Glory to God on high, on earth be peace,
"And love towards men of love—salvation and
    release!"

    Yet, stay before thou dare
      To join that festal throng;

Listen, and mark what gentle air
    First stirred the tide of song;
'Tis not, " the Saviour born in David's home,
" To Whom for power and health obedient worlds should come."

    'Tis not, " the Christ the Lord :"—
        With fixed adoring look
    The quire of Angels caught the word,
        Nor yet their silence broke :
But when they heard the sign, where Christ should be,
In sudden light they shone and heavenly harmony.

    Wrapped in His swaddling bands,
        And in his manger laid,
    The Hope and Glory of all lands
        Is come to the world's aid :
No peaceful home upon His cradle smiled ;
Guests rudely went and came, where slept the Royal Child.

    But where Thou dwellest, Lord,
        No other thought should be,
    Once duly welcomed and adored,
        How should I part with Thee ?

Bethlehem must lose Thee soon; but Thou
  wilt grace
The single heart to be Thy sure abiding place.

>Thee, on the bosom laid
> Of a pure virgin mind,
>In quiet ever, and in shade,
> Shepherd and sage may find;
>They, who have bowed untaught to Nature's
> sway,
>And they who follow Truth along her star-paved
> way.

>The pastoral spirits first
> Approach Thee, Babe divine;
>For they in lowly thoughts are nurst,
> Meet for Thy lowly shrine:
>Sooner than they should miss where Thou
> dost dwell,
>Angels from Heaven will stoop to guide them to
> Thy cell.

>Still, as the day comes round
> For Thee to be revealed,
>By wakeful shepherds Thou art found,
> Abiding in the field.

All through the wintry heaven and chill night air
In music and in light Thou dawnest on their prayer.

    O faint not ye for fear!
      What though your wandering sheep,
    Reckless of what they see and hear,
      Lie lost in wilful sleep?
High Heaven, in mercy to your sad annoy
Still greets you with glad tidings of immortal joy.

    Think on th' eternal home,
      The Saviour left for you;
    Think on the Lord most Holy, come
      To dwell with hearts untrue:
So shall ye tread untired His pastoral ways,
And in the darkness sing your carol of high praise.

                JOHN KEBLE, (1827.)

O THAT THE SALVATION OF ISRAEL WERE COME OUT OF ZION.

EMMANUEL, Thy name we sing,
The Prince of Life, of grace the spring,
The flower of heaven, the star of morn,
Lord of all lords, the Virgin born.   Alleluia.
To Thee with angel hosts we raise
The grateful anthem of our praise,
That Thou art come to save and bless
A world that lies in wickedness.   Alleluia.

For Thee, since first the earth was made,
How many a heart has watched and prayed;
How oft for Thee, with anxious pain,
Have seers and fathers sighed in vain;   Alleluia.
" Ah that from Zion's hill the Lord
" Would come to break our bonds abhorred!
" Ah might we hear the Saviour's voice,
" Our Israel should indeed rejoice."   Alleluia.

Now Thou art here; Thou slumberest,
In lowly manger lulled to rest:

Maker of worlds, an Infant small,
And naked, Thou that clothest all.　Alleluia.
Thou com'st a stranger in the land,
Yet are the heavens in Thy command;
Thou drinkest at a woman's breast,
By angel hosts true God confessed.　Alleluia.

Then fearless I will cling to Thee,
For thou from sorrow makest free;
Thou bindest death, our woes dost bear,
To gladness turning pain and care.　Alleluia.
These lips my lifetime long would raise
Glad alleluias to Thy praise,
And in Thy glorious hall again,
Where time is not, renew the strain.　Alleluia.

THE VIRGIN MARY TO THE CHILD JESUS.

I.

SLEEP, sleep, mine Holy One!
    My flesh, My Lord! what name?
    I do not know
    A name that seemeth not too high or low,
  Too far from me or heaven.
My Jesus, *that* is best! that word being given
By the majestic angel whose command
Was softly as a man's beseeching said,
When I and all the earth appeared to stand
    In the great overflow
Of light celestial from his wings and head.
    Sleep, sleep, my saving One!

II.

And art Thou come for saving, baby-browed
And speechless Being — art Thou come for saving?
The palm that grows beside our door is bowed
By treadings of the low wind from the south,
A restless shadow through the chamber waving:

Upon its bough a bird sings in the sun;
But Thou, with that close slumber on Thy mouth,
Dost seem of wind and sun already weary.
Art come for saving, O my weary One?

III.

Perchance this sleep that shutteth out the dreary
Earth sounds and motions, opens on Thy soul
      High dreams on fire with God;
High songs that make the pathways where they
      roll
More bright than stars do theirs; and visions new
Of Thine eternal Nature's old abode.
    Suffer this mother's kiss,
    Best thing that earthly is,
To glide the music and the glory through,
Nor narrow in Thy dream the broad upliftings
      Of any seraph wing.
Thus noiseless, thus. Sleep, sleep, my dream-
      ing One!

IV.

The slumber of His lips meseems to run
Through *my* lips to mine heart,—to all its shift-
      ings
Of sensual life, bringing contrariousness
In a great calm. I feel, I could lie down
As Moses did, and die,—and then live most.

I am 'ware of you, heavenly Presences,
That stand with your peculiar light unlost,
Each forehead with a high thought for a crown,
Unsunned i' the sunshine! I am 'ware. Ye throw
No shade against the wall! How motionless
Ye round me with your living statuary,
While through your whiteness, in and outwardly,
Continual thoughts of God appear to go,
Like light's soul in itself. I bear, I bear,
To look upon the dropt lids of Your eyes,
Though their external shining testifies
To that beatitude within, which were
Enough to blast an eagle at his sun.
I fall not on my sad clay face before ye,—
  I look on His. I know
My spirit which dilateth with the woe
  Of His mortality,
  May well contain Your glory.
  Yea, drop your lids more low.
Ye are but fellow-worshippers with me!
  Sleep, sleep, my worshipped One!

v.

We sate among the stalls at Bethlehem.
The dumb kine from their fodder turning them,
  Softened their hornéd faces
  To almost human gazes
  Toward the newly Born.

The simple shepherds from the star-lit brooks
    Brought visionary looks,
As yet in their astonied hearing rung
    The strange, sweet angel-tongue.
The magi of the East, in sandals worn,
    Knelt reverent, sweeping round,
With long, pale beards, their gifts upon the ground,
    The incense, myrrh, and gold
These baby hands were impotent to hold.
So, let all earthlies and celestials wait
    Upon Thy royal state.
    Sleep, sleep, my kingly One.

VI.

I am not proud—meek angels, ye invest
New meeknesses to hear such utterance rest
On mortal lips,—" I am not proud "—*not proud!*
Albeit in my flesh God sent his Son,
Albeit over Him my head is bowed
As others bow before Him, still mine heart
Bows lower than their knees. O centuries
That roll, in vision, your futurities
    My future grave athwart,—
Whose murmurs seem to reach me while I keep
    Watch o'er this sleep,—
Say of me as the Heavenly said—' Thou art
The blessedest of women!'—blessedest,
Not holiest, not noblest—no high name,

Whose height misplaced may pierce me like a
    shame,
When I sit meek in heaven!
                  For me, for me,
God knows that I am feeble like the rest!—
I often wandered forth more child than maiden,
Among the midnight hills of Galilee
        Whose summits looked heaven-laden,
Listening to silence as it seemed to be
God's voice; so soft yet strong—so fain to press
Upon my heart as Heaven did on the height,
And waken up its shadows by a light,
And show its vileness by a holiness.
Then I knelt down most silent like the night,
        Too self-renounced for fears,
Raising my small face to the boundless blue
Whose stars did mix and tremble in my tears.
God heard *them* falling after—with his dew.

VII.

So, seeing my corruption, can I see
This Incorruptible now born of me,
This fair new Innocence no sun did chance
To shine on, (for even Adam was no child,)
Created from my nature all defiled,
This mystery, from out mine ignorance;—
Nor feel the blindness, stain, corruption, more
Than others do, or *I* did heretofore?—

Can hands wherein such burden pure has been,
Not open with the cry 'unclean, unclean,'
More oft than any else beneath the skies?
      Ah King, ah Christ, ah Son!
The kine, the shepherds, the abaséd wise;
        Must all less lowly wait
        Than I, upon Thy state :—
      Sleep, sleep, my kingly One!

VIII.

Art Thou a King, then? Come, his universe;
      Come; crown me Him a King!
Pluck rays from all such stars as never fling
      Their light where fell a curse,
And make a crowning for this kingly brow!
What is my word?—Each empyreal star
        Sits in a sphere afar
        In shining ambuscade.
      The child-brow, crowned by none,
      Keeps its unchildlike shade.
      Sleep, sleep, my crownless One!

IX.

Unchildlike shade!—No other babe doth wear
An aspect very sorrowful, as thou.—
No small babe-smiles, my watching heart has
    seen,
To float like speech the speechless lips between.

No dovelike cooing in the golden air,
No quick short joys of leaping babyhood.
    Alas, our earthly good
In heaven thought evil, seems too good for
    Thee:
    Yet, sleep, my weary One!

x.

And then the drear sharp tongue of prophecy,
With the dread sense of things which shall be
    done,
Doth smite me inly, like a sword! a sword?
(*That* 'smites the shepherd.') Then I think
    aloud
The words 'despised,'—'rejected,'—every word
Recoiling into darkness as I view
    The DARLING on my knee.
Bright angels—move not!—lest ye stir the cloud
Betwixt my soul and His futurity!
I must not die, with mother's work to do,
    And could not live—and see.

xi.

    It is enough to bear
    This image still and fair—
    This holier in sleep,
    Than a saint at prayer:

This aspect of a child
Who never sinned or smiled;
This Presence in an infant's face;
This sadness most like love,
This love than love more deep.
This weakness like omnipotence
It is so strong to move.
Awful is this watching place,
Awful what I see from hence—
A King, without regalia,
A God, without the thunder,
A child, without the heart for play;
Ay, a Creator, rent asunder
From His first glory and cast away
On His own world, for me alone
To hold in hands created, crying—Son!

XII.

That tear fell not on Thee
Beloved, yet Thou stirrest in Thy slumber!
THOU, stirring not for glad sounds out of number
Which through the vibratory palm trees run
  From summer wind and bird,
  So quickly hast Thou heard
  A tear fall silently?—
  Wak'st Thou, O loving One?

   ELIZABETH BARRETT BROWNING.

HYMN TO THE NAME OF JESUS.

* * * * * * *

COME lovely name! life of our hope!
Lo, we hold our hearts wide ope!
Unlock thy cabinet of day,
Dearest sweet, and come away.
Lo, how the thirsty lands
Gasp for thy golden show'rs, with long-stretch'd hands!
Lo, how the labouring earth,
That hopes to be
All heaven by thee,
Leaps at thy birth!
The attending world, to wait thy rise,
First turn'd to eyes;
And then, not knowing what to do,
Turn'd them to tears, and spent them too.
Come, royal name! and pay the expense
Of all this precious patience:
Oh, come away
And kill the death of this delay.
Oh, see, so many worlds of barren years
Melted and measured out in seas of tears!

Oh, see the weary lids of wakeful hope
(Love's eastern windows) all wide ope
    With curtains drawn,
To catch the daybreak of thy dawn!
Oh, dawn at last, long-look'd-for day!
Take thine own wings and come away.
Lo, where aloft, it comes! It comes, among
The conduct of adoring spirits, that throng
Like diligent bees, and swarm about it.
    Oh, they are wise,
And know what sweets are suck'd from out it.
    It is the hive
    By which they thrive,
Where all their hoard of honey lies.
Lo, where it comes, upon the snowy dove's
Soft back, and brings a bosom big with loves.
Welcome to our dark world thou womb of day!
Unfold thy fair conceptions; and display
The birth of our bright joys.
    Oh, thou compacted
Body of blessings! spirit of souls extracted!
Oh dissipate thy spicy powers,
Cloud of condensed sweets! and break upon us
    In balmy showers!
Oh fill our senses, and take from us
All force of so profane a fallacy,
To think aught sweet but that which smells of
    thee.

Fair flow'ry name! in none but thee,
And thy nectareal fragrancy,
    Hourly there meets
An universal synod of all sweets;
Sweet name! in thy each syllable
A thousand blest Arabias dwell;
A thousand hills of frankincense;
Mountains of myrrh, and beds of spices,
And ten thousand paradises,
The soul that tastes thee, takes from thence.
How many unknown worlds there are
Of comforts, which thou hast in keeping!
How many thousand mercies there
In pity's soft lap lie a-sleeping!
Happy he who has the art
    To awake them,
      And to take them
Home, and lodge them in his heart.
Oh, that it were as it was wont to be,
When thy old friends, on fire all full of thee,
Fought against frowns with smiles; gave glorious
    chase
To persecutions; and against the face
Of death and fiercest dangers, durst with brave
And sober pace march on to meet a grave.
On their bold breasts about the world they bore
    thee;
And to the teeth of hell stood up to teach thee;

In the centre of their inmost souls they wore
  thee,
Where rack and torment striv'd in vain to reach
  thee.
  Little, alas! thought they
Who tore the fair breasts of thy friends,
  Their fury but made way
For thee, and serv'd them in thy glorious ends.
What did their weapons, but with wider pores
Enlarge thy flaming breasted lovers,
  More freely to transpire
  That impatient fire
The heart that hides thee hardly covers?
What did their weapons, but set wide the doors
For thee? fair purple doors of love's devising;
The ruby windows which enrich'd the east
Of thy so oft-repeated rising.
Each wound of theirs was thy new morning,
And re-enthron'd thee in thy rosy nest,
With blush of thine own blood thy day adorning:
It was the wit of love o'erflow'd the bounds
Of wrath, and made the way through all these
  wounds.
Welcome, dear, all-adored name!
  For sure there is no knee
  That knows not thee;
Or if there be such sons of shame,
  Alas! what will they do,

When stubborn rocks shall bow,
And hills hang down their heav'n-saluting heads
    To seek for humble beds
Of dust, where, in the bashful shades of night,
Next to their own low nothing they may lie,
And couch before the dazzling light of thy dread
    Majesty.
They that by love's mild dictate now
    Will not adore thee,
Shall then, with just confusion, bow
    And break before thee.

                RICHARD CRASHAW, (1644.)

KYRIE ELEISON.

LORD, many times I am aweary quite
    Of mine own self, my sin, my vanity—
Yet be not Thou, or I am lost outright,
    Weary of me.

And hate against myself I often bear,
    And enter with myself in fierce debate;
Take Thou my part against myself, nor share
    In that just hate!

Best friends might loathe us, if what things perverse
    We know of our own selves, they also knew;
Lord, Holy One! if Thou who knowest worse
    Shouldst loathe us too!

R. C. TRENCH.

THE SHADOW OF A GREAT ROCK IN A WEARY LAND.

THE pathways of Thy land are little changed
    Since Thou wert there;
The busy world through other ways hath ranged,
    And left these bare.

The rocky path still climbs the glowing steep
    Of Olivet,
Though rains of two millenniums wear it deep,
    Men tread it yet.

Still to the gardens o'er the brook it leads,
    Quiet and low,
Before his sheep the shepherd on it treads,
    His voice they know.

The wild fig throws broad shadows o'er it still,
    As once o'er Thee;
Peasants go home at evening up that hill
    To Bethany.

And as when gazing Thou didst weep o'er them
    From height to height,
The white roofs of discrowned Jerusalem
    Burst on our sight.

These ways were strew'd with garments once and palm,
    Which we tread thus;
Here through Thy triumph on Thou passedst, calm,
    On to Thy cross.

The waves have washed fresh sand upon the shore
    Of Galilee;
But chiselled on the hill-sides evermore
    Thy paths we see.

Man has not changed them in that slumbering land,
    Nor time effaced;
Where Thy feet trod to bless me still may stand;
    All can be traced.

Yet we have traces of Thy footsteps far
    Truer than these;
Where'er the poor and tried and suffering are,
    Thy steps faith sees.

Nor with fond sad regrets Thy steps we trace;
  Thou art not dead!
Our faith is onward till we see Thy face
  And hear Thy tread.

And now wherever meets Thy lowliest band
  In praise and prayer,
There is Thy presence, there Thy Holy Land—
  Thou, Thou art there!

Author of the "Three Wakings."

THY LIGHT IS COME.

How brightly dawns the Morning Star,
With mercy coming from afar!
   The host of heaven rejoices;
O righteous Branch, O Jesse's Rod,
Thou Son of man, and Son of God,
   We too will lift our voices.
      Jesu! Jesu!
Holy, holy, yet most lowly,
   Draw Thou near us:
Great Emmanuel, stoop and hear us.

Though circled by the hosts on high,
He deigned to cast a pitying eye
   Upon his helpless creature;
The whole creation's Head and Lord,
By highest Seraphim adored,
   Assumed our very nature:
      Jesu, grant us,
Through Thy merit, to inherit
   Thy salvation;
Hear, O hear our supplication.

Then will we to the world make known
The love Thou hast to outcasts shown
   In calling them before Thee:
And seek each day to be more meet
To join the throng who at Thy feet
   Unceasingly adore Thee.
      Living, dying,
   From Thy praises, mighty Jesus,
      Shrink we never.
Sing we forth Thy love for ever.

Rejoice, ye heavens; and earth reply:
With praise, ye sinners, fill the sky
   For love so condescending.
Incarnate God, put forth Thy power,
Ride on, ride on, great Conqueror,
   Thy glory wide extending.
      Amen, amen!
   Hallelujah, Hallelujah!
      Praise be given
To Thy name in earth and heaven.

ON A PICTURE OF THE ADORATION OF THE MAGIANS.

LITTLE pomp of earthly state
    On His lowly steps might wait;
    Few the homages and small,
    That the guilty earth at all
Was permitted to accord
To her King and hidden Lord:
Therefore do we set more store
On these few and prize them more;
Dear to us for this account
Is the glory of the Mount,
When bright beams of light did spring
Through the sackcloth covering—
Rays of glory forced their way
Through the garments of decay,
With which, as with a cloak, he had
His divinest splendors clad:
Dear the lavish ointment shed
On His feet and sacred head;
And the high-raised hopes sublime,
And the triumph of the time,

When through Zion's streets the way
Of her peaceful Conqueror lay,
Who, fulfilling ancient fame,
Meek and with salvation came.

But of all this scanty state
That upon his steps might wait,
Dearest are those Magian kings,
With their far-brought offerings.
From what region of the morn
Are ye come, thus travel-worn,
With those boxes pearl-embossed,
Caskets rare, and gifts of cost?
While, your swart attendants wait
At the stable's outer gate,
And the camels lift their head
High above the lowly shed;
Or are seen, a long-drawn train,
Winding down into the plain,
From beyond the light-blue line
Of the hills in distance fine.
Dear for your own sake, whence are ye?
Dearer for the mystery
That is round you—on what skies
Gazing, saw you first arise
Through the darkness that clear star,
Which has marshalled you so far,
Even unto this strawy tent—

Dancing up the Orient?
Shall we name you kings indeed,
Or is this our idle creed?—
Kings of Seba, with the gold
And the incense long foretold?
Would the Gentile world by you
First-fruits pay of tribute due?
Or have Israel's scattered race,
From their unknown hiding-place,
Sent to claim their part and right
In the child new-born to-night?

But although we may not guess
Of your lineage, not the less
We the self-same gifts would bring,
For a spiritual offering.
May the frankincense, in air
As it climbs, instruct our prayer,
That it ever upward tend,
Ever struggle to ascend,
Leaving earth, yet ere it go
Fragrance rich diffuse below.
As the myrrh is bitter-sweet,
So in us may such things meet,
As unto the mortal taste
Bitter seeming, yet at last
Shall to them who try be known
To have sweetness of their own—

Tears for sin, which sweeter far
Than the world's mad laughters are;
Desires, that in their dying give
Pain, but die that we may live.
And the gold from Araby—
Fitter symbol who could see
Of the love which, thrice refined,
Love to God and to our kind,
Duly tendered, he will call
Choices sacrifice of all?

Thus so soon as far apart
From the proud world, in our heart,
As in stable dark defiled,
There is born the Eternal Child,
May to Him, the spirit's Kings
Yield their choicest offerings;
May the Affections, Reason, Will,
Wait upon Him to fulfil
His behests, and early pay
Homage to His natal day.

R. C. Trench.

THE MOUNT OF OLIVES.

"He went out into a mountain to pray, and continued all night in prayer to God." *St. Luke* vi. 12.

THOU didst love the evening hours,
    Saviour of the world and me,
And the closing of the flowers
    Brought welcome rest to Thee,
As the hireling gladly sees
The long shadows of the trees.

Rest, but not on beds of down,
    Curtained close in soft repose;
Thou didst seek the mountain's crown;
    Where the shady olive grows,
Thou didst find a place of prayer,
Commune with Thy Father there.

Ah, methinks I see Thee now,
    Climbing, late, the mountain side;
Cool night-breezes fan Thy brow,
    Days long cares in shadows hide:
Far below the eastern steep
Salem lies in double sleep!

All day long those hands of Thine
   Mercy's almoners have been;
All day long those eyes Divine
   Sights of want and woe have seen;
All day long those ears have heard
Many a harsh and sinful word.

Rest Thee, Saviour, rest Thee now!
   Let Thy weary eyelids close;
On the lonely mountain's brow
   Nought shall break Thy calm repose;
Of Thy slumbers shall be born
Strength for toil with coming morn.

Angel hands Thy couch shall spread
   On the green and mossy sward;
At Thy feet and at Thy head
   Cherubim keep watch and ward:
Bright, like his at Luz shall be
Midnight visions unto Thee!

Nay—He rests not—see Him there,
   Kneeling low upon the sod,
All the burden of His prayer
   Pouring forth as man to God;
Far away from earthly jars,
In the clear, calm light of stars.

For Himself He prays awhile,—
   Strength to do His will on earth;
He whose spirit knew no guile,
   Bore no taint of sinful birth;
Strength to bear His Father's frown,
Grace to spurn the proffered crown.

Then for those few simple sheep,
   Earnest of His future fold,
Fervent yearnings upward leap,
   Faith and Hope for them grow bold;
Angel censors through the air
Waft the perfume of His prayer.

But the first gray light of morning
   Pierces now the Olive shade;
Early birds with gentle warning,
   Carol through the leafy glade;
All unrested, save by prayer,
Jesus drinks the morning air.

Saviour! let Thy evening hours
   Dear to us, Thy children, be;
With claspéd hands, as folded flowers,
   Praying earnestly to Thee,
Let our vesper-worship rise
Incense-like before Thine eyes;—

Then, when that dark even-tide
    Closes in our life's long day,
And, like some steep mountain-side,
    Frowns the last and lonesome way,
Bright to us that path shall be,
Found alone, O Lord, with Thee.
C. L. Ford.

GETHSEMANE.

The night is dark—behold, the shade was deeper
   In the still garden of Gethsemane,
When the calm Voice awoke the weary sleeper,
"Couldst thou not watch an hour alone with Me?"

O thou, so weary of thy self-denials,
   And so impatient of thy little cross,
Is it so hard to bear thy daily trials—
   To count all earthly things a gainful loss?

What if thou always sufferest tribulation?
   What if thy Christian warfare never cease?
The gaining of the quiet habitation
   Shall gather thee to everlasting peace.

Here are we all to suffer, walking lonely
   The path that Jesus once Himself hath gone;
Watch thou this hour in trustful patience only,
   This one dark hour before the eternal dawn:

And He will come in His own time from Heaven,
　To set His earnest-hearted children free;
Watch only through this dark and painful even,
　And the bright morning yet will break for thee.

FOR GOOD FRIDAY.

"Is it nothing to you, all ye that pass by? Behold, and see if there be any sorrow like unto My sorrow."

JESUS, mighty Sufferer! say,
How shall we this dreadful day
Near Thee draw and to Thee pray?

We whose proneness to forget
Thy dear love on Olivet,
Bathed Thy brow with bloody sweat;—

We, who still in thought and deed
Often hold the bitter reed
To Thee, in Thy time of need;—

Canst Thou pardon us, and pray,
As for those who on this day
Took Thy precious life away?

Yes, Thy blood is all my plea;
It was shed, and shed for me,
Therefore to Thy Cross I flee.

At Thy feet, in dust and shame,
I dare breathe Thy holy Name,
And Thy great salvation claim.

Jesu, deign in love to take
Pity on my soul, and make
This day bright for Thy dear sake.
                                  Amen.

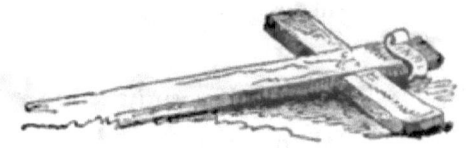

THE POWER OF THE CROSS.

"And they that are Christ's have crucified the flesh with the affections and lusts." Gal. v.

 CROSS, we hail thy bitter reign;
   O come, thou well-belovéd guest,
Whose sorest sufferings work not pain,
   Whose heaviest burden is but rest.
For is not our Redeemer bound
   In closest ties of love to those
Who faithful to the Cross are found
   Through ceaseless tears, through saddest woes?

Pledge of our glorious home afar,
   Thee, holy sign, with joy we take,
Sign of a peace life cannot mar,
   Of just content death cannot shake:
The sign, how truth, once crucified
   Now throned in majesty doth reign,
How love is blest and glorified,
   Which here on earth was mocked and slain.

Their names are writ in words of light
    Who here on earth their Lord confessed:
They hear the Bridegroom's cry at night,
    Come to my marriage feast, ye blest.
Who then would faint, nor gladly share
    In Christ's reproach, in want or pain?
The bitterest death who would not dare
    With joy, the martyr's crown to gain?

        CATHERINE WINKWORTH, "*Lyr. Ger.*"

AND THE PEOPLE STOOD BEHOLDING.

SWEET the moments, rich in blessing,
   Which before the Cross we spend,
Life, and health, and peace possessing
   From the sinner's dying Friend.
Rest we here, for ever viewing
   Mercy's streaming fount of blood;
Precious drops, our soul bedewing,
   Plead and claim our peace with God.

Truly blessèd is the station;
   Low before His Cross we lie,
While we see divine compassion
   Beaming from His earnest eye:
Here we feel our sins forgiven,
   While upon the Lamb we gaze,
And our thoughts are all of heaven,
   And our hearts o'erflow with praise.

For Thy sorrows we adore Thee,
    For the pains that wrought our peace;
Gracious Saviour, we implore Thee,
    In our souls Thy love increase:
Still in ceaseless contemplation
    Fix our hearts and eyes on Thee,
Till we taste Thy full salvation,
    And unveiled Thy glories see.   Amen.

BRYDGES.

JESUS OUR LOVE IS CRUCIFIED.

HIS Mother cannot reach His face;
  She stands in helplessness beside,
  Her heart is martyred with her
    Son's,—
  Jesus, our Love, is crucified!

What was Thy crime, my dearest Lord?
  By earth, by heaven, Thou hast been tried,
And guilty found of too much love;—
  Jesus, our Love, is crucified!

Found guilty of excess of love,
  It was Thine own sweet will that tied
Thee tighter far than helpless nails;—
  Jesus, our Love, is crucified!

O come and mourn with me awhile;
  See Mary calls us to her side;
O come and let us mourn with her;—
  Jesus, our Love, is crucified!

Have we no tears to shed for Him,
    While soldiers scoff and Jews deride?
Ah! look how patiently He hangs,—
    Jesus, our Love, is crucified!

O break, O break, hard heart of mine!
    Thy weak self-love and guilty pride
His Pilate and His Judas were;
    Jesus, our Love, is crucified!

Come, take thy stand beneath the Cross,
    And let the Blood from out that Side
Fall gently on thee drop by drop;
    Jesus, our Love, is crucified!

A broken heart, a fount of tears,—
    Ask, and they will not be denied;
A broken heart love's cradle is;
    Jesus, our Love, is crucified!

O Love of God! O Son of Man!
    In this dread act Your strength is tried;
And victory remains with love,
    For He, our Love, is crucified!

FABER.

NOW THERE STOOD BY THE CROSS OF JESUS HIS MOTHER.

AT the Cross her station keeping,
Stood the mournful Mother weeping,
  Where He hung, the dying Lord;
For her soul of joy bereavéd,
Bowed with anguish, deeply grievéd,
  Felt the sharp and piercing sword.

O how sad and sore distresséd—
Nor was she, that Mother blesséd
  Of the sole begotten One;
Deep the woe of her affliction
When she saw the crucifixion
  Of her ever-glorious Son.

Who on Christ's dear Mother gazing,
Pierced by anguish so amazing,
  Born of woman would not weep?
Who on Christ's dear Mother thinking,
Such a cup of sorrow drinking,
  Would not share her sorrows deep?

For His people's sins chastiséd
She beheld her Son despiséd,
   Scourged and crowned with thorny wreath;
Saw Him then from judgment taken,
Mocked by foes, by friends forsaken,
   Till He gave His soul to death.

Jesu, may such deep devotion
Stir in me the same emotion,
   Fount of love, Redeemer kind,
That my heart, fresh ardour gaining,
And a purer love attaining,
   May with Thee acceptance find. Amen.

LIGHT FROM THE CROSS.

"And I, if I be lifted up from the earth, will draw all men unto Me."

    LAMP of Life! that on the bloody Cross
      Dost hang, the Beacon of our wandering race,
To guide us homeward to our resting-place,
And save our best wealth from eternal loss!
So purge my inward sight from earthly dross,
   That, fix'd upon Thy Cross, or near or far,
In all the storms this weary bark that toss,
   (Whate'er be lost in that tempestuous war,)
   Thee I retain, my Compass and my Star!
That, when arrived upon the wish'd-for strand,
   I pass of death th' irrevocable bar,
And at the gate of Heaven trembling stand,
The everlasting doors may open wide,
And give Thee to my sight, God glorified!
CHARLES DYSON, (1816.)

JESU.

JESU is in my heart; his sacred name
Is deeply carved there. But, th' other week,
A great affliction broke the little frame,
Even all to pieces; which I went to seek.
And first I found the corner where was *I*;
After, where *ES*; and next, where *U* was graved.
When I had got these parcels, instantly
I sat me down to spell them; and perceived
That, to my *broken* heart, he was *I EASE YOU*;
And, to my *whole*, is *JESU*.

GEORGE HERBERT.

ECCE AGNUS DEI!

BEHOLD the Lamb!
Oh! Thou for sinners slain,—
Let it not be in vain,
 That Thou hast died:
Thee for my Saviour let me take,—
Thee,—Thee alone my refuge make,—
 Thy piercéd side!

Behold the Lamb!
Archangels,—fold your wings,—
Seraphs,—hush all the strings
 Of million lyres:
The Victim, veiled on earth, in love,—
Unveiled—enthroned,—adored above,
 All heaven admires!

Behold the Lamb!
Drop down, ye glorious skies,—
He dies,—He dies,—He dies,—
 For man once lost!
Yet lo! He lives,—He lives,—He lives,—
And to His Church Himself He gives,—
 Incarnate Host!

Behold the Lamb!
All hail,—Eternal Word!—
Thou universal Lord,—
    Purge out our leaven:
Clothe us with godliness and good,
Feed us with Thy celestial food,—
    Manna from heaven!

Behold the Lamb!
Saints, wrapt in blissful rest,—
Souls,—waiting to be blest,—
    O Lord,—how long!
Thou church on earth, o'erwhelmed with fears,
Still in this vale of woe and tears,
    Swell the full song.

Behold the Lamb!
Worthy is He alone,
To sit upon the throne
    Of God above!
One with the Ancient of all days,—
One with the Paraclete in praise,—
    All light,—all love!

EGERTON BRYDGES.

AT THE FOOT OF THE CROSS.

BENEATH my cross I lay me down,
And mourn to see Thy bloody crown;
Love drops in blood from every vein;
Love is the spring of all His pain.

Here, Jesus, I shall ever stay,
And spend my longing heart away,
Think on Thy bleeding wounds and pain,
And contemplate Thy woes again.

The rage of Satan and of sin,
Of foes without, and fears within,
Shall ne'er my conquering soul remove
Or from Thy Cross or from Thy love.

Secured from harms beneath Thy shade,
Here death and hell shall ne'er invade;
Nor Sinai, with its thundering noise,
Shall e'er disturb my happier joys.

O unmolested happy rest!
Where inward fears are all supprest;
Here I shall love, and live secure,
And patiently my cross endure.
        WILLIAM WILLIAMS, (1772.)

THY WILL, NOT MINE.

"Father, if Thou be willing, remove this cup from Me: nevertheless not My will, but Thine, be done." *St. Luke* xxii. 42.

LORD my God, do Thou Thy holy will—
 I will lie still—
I will not stir, lest I forsake Thine arm,
 And break the charm,
Which lulls me, clinging to my Father's breast,
 In perfect rest.

Wild Fancy, peace! thou must not me beguile
 With thy false smile:
I know thy flatteries and thy cheating ways;
 Be silent, Praise,
Blind guide with siren voice, and blinding all
 That hear thy call.

Come Self-devotion, high and pure,
Thoughts that in thankfulness endure,
Though dearest hopes are faithless found,

And dearest hearts are bursting round.
Come, Resignation, spirit meek,
And let me kiss thy placid cheek,
And read in thy pale eye serene
Their blessing, who by faith can wean
Their hearts from sense, and learn to love
God only, and the joys above.

They say, who know the life divine,
And upward gaze with eagle eyne,
That by each golden crown on high,
Rich with celestial jewelry,
Which for our Lord's Redeemed is set,
There hangs a radiant coronet,
All gemmed with pure and living light,
Too dazzling for a sinner's sight,
Prepared for virgin souls, and them
Who seek the martyr's diadem.

Nor deem, who to that bliss aspire,
Must win their way through blood and fire.
The writhings of a wounded heart
Are fiercer than a foeman's dart.
Oft in Life's stillest shades reclining,
In Desolation unrepining,
Without a hope on earth to find
A mirror in an answering mind,
Meek souls there are, who little dream,

Their daily strife an Angel's theme,
Or that the rod they take so calm
Shall prove in Heaven a martyr's palm.

And there are souls that seem to dwell
Above the earth,—so rich a spell
Floats round their steps, where'er they move,
From hopes fulfilled and mutual love.
Such, if on high their thoughts are set,
Nor in the stream the source forget,
If prompt to quit the bliss they know,
Following the Lamb where'er He go,
By purest pleasures unbeguiled
To idolize or wife or child;
Such wedded souls our God shall own
For faultless virgins round His throne.

Thus everywhere we find our suffering God,
   And where He trod
May set our steps: the Cross on Calvary
   Uplifted high
Beams on the martyr host, a beacon light
   In open fight.

To the still wrestlings of the lonely heart
   He doth impart
The virtue of His midnight agony,
   Where none is nigh,

Save God and one good angel to assuage
      The tempest's rage.

Mortal! if life smile on thee, and thou find
      All to thy mind,
Think, who did once from Heaven to Hell descend
      Thee to befriend:
So shalt thou dare forego, at His dear call,
      Thy best, thine all.

"O Father! not My will, but Thine be done"—
      So speaks the Son.
Be this our charm, mellowing Earth's ruder noise
      Of griefs and joys;
That we may cling forever to Thy breast
      In perfect rest.

KEBLE.

TOUCHED WITH A FEELING OF OUR INFIRMITIES.

When wounded sore, the stricken soul
   Lies bleeding and unbound,
One only Hand, a pierced Hand,
   Can salve the sinner's wound.

When sorrow swells the laden breast,
   And tears of anguish flow,
One only Heart, a broken Heart,
   Can feel the sinner's woe.

When penitence has wept in vain
   Over some foul dark spot,
One only stream, a stream of blood,
   Can wash away the blot.

'Tis Jesus' blood that washes white,
   This Hand that brings relief,
This Heart that's touched with all our joys,
   And feeleth for our grief.

Lift up Thy bleeding Hand, O Lord,
  Unseal that cleansing tide;
We have no shelter from our sin
  But in Thy wounded side.

                C. F. ALEXANDER.

HE WAS DESPISED AND REJECTED OF MEN.

IS it not strange, the darkest hour
    That ever dawned on sinful earth
Should touch the heart with softer power
    For comfort, than an angel's mirth?
That to the Cross the mourner's eye should turn
Sooner than where the stars of Christmas burn?

Sooner than where the Easter sun
    Shines glorious on yon open grave,
And to and fro the tidings run,
    "Who died to heal, is ris'n to save?"
Sooner than where upon the Saviour's friends
The very Comforter in light and love descends?

Yet it is so: for duly there
    The bitter herbs of earth are set,
Till tempered by the Saviour's prayer,
    And with the Saviour's life-blood wet,
They turn to sweetness, and drop holy balm,
Soft as imprisoned martyr's death-bed calm.

All turn to sweet—but most of all,
   That bitterest to the lip of pride,
When hopes presumptuous fade and fall,
   Or Friendship scorns us, duly tried,
Or Love, the flower that closes up for fear
When rude and selfish spirits breathe too near.

Then like a long-forgotten strain
   Comes sweeping o'er the heart forlorn
What sunshine hours had taught in vain
   Of JESUS suffering shame and scorn,
As in all lowly hearts He suffers still,
While we triumphant ride and have the world at
   will.

His piercéd hands in vain would hide
   His face from rude reproachful gaze,
His ears are open to abide
   The wildest storm the tongue can raise,
He who with one rough word, some early day,
Their idol world and them shall sweep for aye away.

But we by Fancy may assuage
   The festering sore by Fancy made,
Down in some lonely hermitage
   Like wounded pilgrims safely laid,
Where gentlest breezes whisper souls distressed,
That Love yet lives, and Patience shall find rest.

O! sname beyond the bitterest thought
    That evil spirits ever framed,
That sinners know what Jesus wrought,
    Yet feel their haughty hearts untamed—
That souls in refuge, holding by the Cross,
Would wince and fret at this world's little loss.

Lord of my heart, by Thy last cry
    Let not Thy blood on earth be spent—
Lo, at Thy feet I fainting lie,
    Mine eyes upon Thy wounds are bent;
Upon Thy streaming wounds my weary eyes
Wait like the parched earth on April skies.

Wash me, and dry these bitter tears,
    O let my heart no further roam,
'Tis Thine by vows, and hopes, and fears,
    Long since—O call Thy wanderer home;
To that dear home, safe in Thy wounded side,
Where only broken hearts their sin and shame
    may hide.
KEBLE.

JESUS CRUCIFIED.

MY Lord, my love was crucified,
    He all the pains did bear;
But in the sweetness of His rest
    He makes His servants share.
How sweetly rest Thy saints above
    Which in Thy bosom lie!
The Church below doth rest in hope
    Of that felicity.

Thou, Lord, who daily feed'st Thy sheep,
    Mak'st them a weekly feast;
Thy flocks meet in their several folds
    Upon this day of rest:
Welcome and dear unto my soul
    Are these sweet feasts of love:
But what a Sabbath shall I keep
    When I shall rest above!

I bless Thy wise and wondrous love,
    Which binds us to be free;
Which makes us leave our earthly snares,
    That we may come to Thee!

I come, I wait, I hear, I pray!
    Thy footsteps, Lord, I trace!
I sing to think this is the way
    Unto my Saviour's face!

JOHN MASON, (1683.)

THE ENTOMBMENT.

"And Joseph wrapped the body in a clean linen cloth, and laid it in his own new tomb, which he had hewn out in the rock."

REST of the weary! Thou
  Thyself art resting now,
Where lowly in Thy sepulchre Thou
    liest:
 From out her deathly sleep
 My soul doth start to weep
So sad a wonder, that Thou Saviour diest!

  Thy bitter anguish o'er,
  To this dark tomb they bore
Thee, Life of life,—Thee, Lord of all creation!
  The hollow rocky cave
  Must serve Thee for a grave,
Who wast Thyself the Rock of our Salvation!

  O Prince of Life! I know
  That when I too lie low,

Thou wilt at last my soul from death awaken;
    Wherefore I will not shrink
    From the grave's rueful brink;
The heart that trusts in Thee shall ne'er be shaken.

    To me the darksome tomb
    Is but a narrow room,
Where I may rest in peace, from sorrow free.
    Thy death shall give me power
    To cry in that dark hour,
O Death, O Grave, where is your victory?

    The grave can nought destroy,
    Only the flesh can die,
And e'en the body triumphs o'er decay;
    Cloth'd by Thy wondrous might
    In robes of dazzling light,
The flesh shall burst the grave at the last Day.

    My Jesus, day by day,
    Help me to watch and pray,
Beside the tomb where in my heart Thou'rt laid.
    Thy bitter death shall be
    My constant memory,
My guide at last into Death's awful shade.
    CATHERINE WINKWORTH, "*Lyr. Ger.*"

MORS CHRISTI.

AND am I here, and my Redeemer gone?
Can He be dead, and is not my life done?
Was He tormented in excesse of measure,
And doe I live yet? and yet live in pleasure?
Alas! could sinners find out ne'r a one
More fit than Thee for them to spit upon?
Did Thy cheekes entertaine a traytor's lips?
Was Thy deare body scourg'd and torne with whips,
So that the guiltlesse blood came trickling after?
And did Thy fainting browes sweat blood and water?
Wert Thou (Lord) hang'd upon the cursed tree?
O world of griefe! and was this all for me?
Burst forth, my teares, into a world of sorrow,

And let my nights of griefe find ne'r a morrow :
Since Thou art dead (Lord) grant Thy servant room
Within his heart to build Thy heart a tombe.

       FRANCIS QUARLES.

MY FLESH ALSO SHALL REST IN HOPE.

"As for Thee also, by the blood of Thy covenant I have sent forth Thy prisoners out of the pit wherein is no water." *Zech.* ix. 11.

AT length the worst is o'er, and Thou art laid
 Deep in Thy darksome bed;
All still and cold beneath yon dreary stone
 Thy sacred form is gone;
Around those lips where power and mercy hung
 The dews of death have clung;
The dull earth o'er Thee, and Thy foes around,
Thou sleep'st a silent corse, in funeral fetters wound.

Sleep'st Thou indeed? or is Thy spirit fled,
 At large among the dead?
Whether in Eden bowers Thy welcome voice
 Wake Abraham to rejoice,
Or in some drearier scene Thine eye controls
 The thronging band of souls;

That, as Thy blood on earth, Thine agony
Might set the shadowy realm from sin and sor-
    row free.

Where'er Thou roam'st, one happy soul, we
    know
    Seen at Thy side in woe,
Waits on Thy triumph—even as all the blest
    With him and Thee shall rest.
Each on his cross, by Thee we hang awhile,
    Watching Thy patient smile,
'Till we have learned to say, " 'Tis justly done
Only in glory, Lord, Thy sinful servant own."

Soon wilt Thou take us to Thy tranquil bower
    To rest one little hour,
Till Thine elect are numbered, and the grave
    Call Thee to come and save:
Then on Thy bosom borne shall we descend,
    Again with earth to blend,
Earth all refined with bright supernal fires,
Tinctured with holy blood, and winged with pure
    desires:

Meanwhile, with every son and saint of Thine
    Along the glorious line,
Sitting by turns beneath Thy sacred feet
    We'll hold communion sweet,

Know them by look and voice, and thank them all
   For helping us in thrall,
For words of hope, and bright examples given
To show through moonless skies that there is light in Heaven.

O come that day, when in the restless heart
   Earth shall resign her part,
When in the grave with Thee my limbs shall rest,
   My soul with Thee be blest!
But stay, presumptuous—CHRIST with thee abides
   In the rock's dreary sides;
He from the stone will wring celestial dew
If but the prisoner's heart be faithful found and true.

When tears are spent, and thou art left alone
   With ghosts of blessings gone,
Think thou art taken from the cross, and laid
   In JESUS' burial shade;
Take Moses' rod, the rod of prayer, and call
   Out of the rocky wall
The fount of holy blood; and life on high
Thy grovelling soul that feels so desolate and dry.

Prisoner of Hope thou art—look up and sing
    In hope of promised spring.
As in the pit his father's darling lay
    Beside the desert way,
And knew not how, but knew his GOD would save
    Even from that living grave,
So buried with our LORD, will close our eyes
To the decaying world, till angels bid us rise.
KEBLE.

HE GIVETH HIS BELOVED SLEEP.

I.

OF all the thoughts of God, that are
Borne inward unto souls afar,
 Along the Psalmist's music deep—
Now tell me if that any is,
For gift of grace surpassing this—
 "He giveth His beloved sleep"?

His dews drop mutely on the hill—
His cloud above it saileth still—
 Though on its slope men toil and reap;
More softly than the dew is shed,
Or cloud is floated overhead,
 "He giveth His beloved sleep."

And friends, dear friends! when shall it be,
That this low breath is gone from me—
 When round my bier ye come to weep;

Let one, most loving of you all,
Say —" Not a tear must o'er her fall,
" He giveth His beloved sleep."

II.

What would we give to our beloved?
The hero's heart to be unmoved—
   The poet's star-tuned harp to sweep—
The senate's shout to patriot vows—
The monarch's crown to light the brows?
   " He giveth His beloved sleep."

" Sleep soft, beloved ! " we sometimes say,
But have no power to charm away
   Sad dreams that through the eyelids creep;
But never doleful dream again
Shall break their happy slumber, when
   " He giveth His beloved sleep."

O earth, so full of dreary noise!
O men, with wailing in your voice!
   O delvèd gold, the wailer's heap!
O strife, O curse, that o'er it fall!
God makes a silence through you all,
   And giveth his beloved sleep!

Yea! men may wonder while they scan—
A living, thinking, feeling man
  In such a rest his heart to keep!
But angels say—and through the word,
I ween, their blessed smile is heard—
  "He giveth His beloved sleep."

        ELIZABETH BARRETT BROWNING.

THE FOE BEHIND, THE DEEP BEFORE.

THE foe behind, the deep before,
    Our hosts have dared and past the sea;
    And Pharaoh's warriors strew the shore,
    And Israel's ransomed tribes are free.
Lift up, lift up your voices now!
The whole wide world rejoices now!
The Lord hath triumphed gloriously!
The Lord shall reign victoriously!
    Happy morrow
    Turning sorrow
       Into peace and mirth!
    Bondage ending,
    Love descending,
       O'er the earth!
    Souls assuring,
    Guards securing,
       Watch His earthly prison:
    Seals are shattered,
    Guards are scattered,
       Christ hath risen!

No longer must the mourners weep,
   Nor call departed Christians dead;
For death is hallowed into sleep,
   And every grave becomes a bed.
      Now once more,
      Eden's door
Open stands to mortal eyes;
For Christ hath risen, and men shall rise:
      Now at last,
      Old things past,
Hope and joy and peace begin;
For Christ hath won, and man shall win.

It is not exile, rest on high:
   It is not sadness, peace from strife:
To fall asleep is not to die;
   To dwell with Christ is better life.
      Where our banner leads us,
         We may safely go:
      Where our Chief precedes us,
         We may face the foe.
      His right arm is o'er us,
         He will guide us through;
      Christ hath gone before us;
         Christians! follow you!

            JOHN MASON NEALE, (1851.)

EASTER DAY.

A PATHWAY opens from the tomb,
    The grave's a grave no more!
Stoop down; look into that sweet
    room;
Pass through the unseal'd door:
Linger a moment by the bed,
Where lay but yesterday the Church's Head.

What is there there to make thee fear?
    A folded chamber-vest,
Akin to that which thou shalt wear,
    When for thy slumber drest;
Two gentle angels sitting by—
How sweet a room, methinks, wherein to lie!

No gloomy vault, no charnel cell,
    No emblem of decay,
No solemn sound of passing bell,
    To say, "He's gone away;"—
But angel-whispers soft and clear,
And He, the risen Jesus, standing near.

"Why weepest thou? Whom seekest thou?"
  'Tis not the gardener's voice,
But His to whom all knees shall bow,
  In whom all hearts rejoice;
The voice of Him who yesterday,
Within that rock was Death's resistless prey.

"Why weepest thou? whom seekest thou?
  The living with the dead?"
Take young spring flowers and deck thy brow,
  For life with joy is wed:
The grave is now the grave no more;
Why fear to pass that bridal-chamber door?

Take flowers and strew them all around
  The room where Jesus lay:
But softly tread; 'tis hallowed ground,
  And this is Easter-day.
"The Lord is risen," as He said,
And thou shalt rise with Him, thy risen Head.

RESURRECTION.

"And when the Lord saw her, He had compassion on her, and said unto her, Weep not. And He came and touched the bier; and they that bare him stood still. And He said, Young man, I say unto thee, Arise. *St. Luke*, vii. 13, 14.

HO says the wan autumnal sun
    Beams with too faint a smile
  To light up nature's face again,
  And, though the year be on the wane,
With thoughts of spring the heart beguile?

Waft him, thou soft September breeze,
    And gently lay him down
  Within some circling woodland wall,
  Where bright leaves reddening ere they fall,
    Wave gaily o'er the waters brown.

And let some graceful arch be there
    With wreathed mullions proud,

With burnished ivy for its screen,
And moss, that glows as fresh and green
   As though beneath an April cloud.

Who says the widow's heart must break,
   The childless mother sink?—
A kinder, truer voice I hear,
Which even beside that mournful bier
   Whence parent's eyes would hopeless shrink,

Bids weep no more—O heart bereft,
   How strange, to thee, that sound!
A widow o'er her only son,
Feeling more bitterly alone
   For friends that press officious round.

Yet is the voice of comfort heard,
   For Christ has touched the bier—
The bearers wait with wondering eye,
The swelling bosom dares not sigh,
   But all is still, 'twixt hope and fear.

Even such an awful soothing calm
   We sometimes see alight
On Christian mourners, while they wait
In silence, by some church-yard gate,
   Their summons to the holy rite.

And such the tones of love, which break
    The stillness of that hour,
Quelling th' embittered spirit's strife—
"The Resurrection and the Life
  "Am I: believe, and die no more."—

Unchanged that voice—and though not yet
    The dead sit up and speak,
Answering its call; we gladlier rest
Our darlings on earth's quiet breast,
    And our hearts feel they must not break.

Far better they should sleep awhile
    Within the church's shade,
Nor wake, until new heaven, new earth,
Meet for their young immortal birth
    For their abiding place be made,

Than wander back to life, and lean
    On our frail love once more.
'Tis sweet, as year by year we lose
Friends out of sight, in faith to muse
    How grows in Paradise our store.

Then pass, ye mourners, cheerly on,
    Through prayer unto the tomb,

Still, as ye watch life's falling leaf,
Gathering from every loss and grief
   Hope of new spring and endless home.

Then cheerly to your work again
   With hearts new-braced and set
To run, untired, love's blessed race,
As meet for those, who face to face
   Over the grave their Lord have met.

KEBLE.

DEAR SAVIOUR OF A DYING WORLD.

DEAR Saviour of a dying world,
   Where grief and change must be,
In the new grave where Thou wast
     laid,
   My heart lies down with Thee.
Oh, not in cold despair of joy,
   Or weariness of pain,
But from a hope that shall not die,
   To rise and live again.

I would arise in all Thy strength
   Thy place on earth to fill,
To work out all my time of war
   With love's unflinching will;
Firm against every doubt of Thee
   For all my future way—
To walk in Heaven's eternal light
   Throughout the changing day.

Ah, such a day as Thou shalt own
   When suns have ceased to shine!

A day of burdens borne by Thee,
   And work that all was Thine.
Speed Thy bright rising in my heart,
   Thy righteous kingdom speed,—
Till my whole life in concord say,
   " The Lord is risen indeed."

Oh for an impulse from Thy love
   With every coming breath,
To sing that sweet undying song
   Amid the wrecks of death!
A "hail!" to every mortal pang
   That bids me take my right
To glory in the blessed life
   Which Thou hast brought to light.

I long to see the hallowed earth
   In new creation rise,—
To find the germs of Eden hid
   Where its fallen beauty lies,—
To feel the spring-tide of a soul
   By one deep love set free;
Made meet to lay aside her dust,
   And be at home with Thee.

And then—there shall be yet an end—
   An end now full to bless!

How dear to those who watch for Thee
   With human tenderness!
Then shall the saying come to pass
   That makes our home complete,
And, rising from the conquered grave,
   Thy parted ones shall meet.

Yes—they shall meet, and face to face
   By heart to heart be known,
Clothed with Thy likeness, Lord of life,
   And perfect in their own.
For this corruptible must rise,
   From its corruption free,
And this frail mortal must put on
   Thine immortality.

Shine, then, Thou Resurrection Light,
   Upon our sorrows shine;
The fulness of Thy joys be ours,
   As all our griefs were Thine.
Now, in this changing, dying life
   Our faded hopes restore,
Till, in Thy triumph perfected,
   We taste of death no more.

A. L. WARING.

EASTER.

RISE, heart! thy Lord is risen. Sing
        His praise
        Without delays,
Who takes thee by the hand, that thou likewise
        With Him mayst rise;
That as thy death calcined thee to dust,
His life may make thee gold; and, much more, just.

Awake, my lute, and struggle for thy part
        With all thy art.
The cross taught all wood to resound his name,
        Who bore the same.
His stretched sinews taught all strings what key
Is best to celebrate this most high day.

Consort both heart and lute, and twist a song
        Pleasant and long:
Or, since all music is but three parts vied,
        And multiplied;

O let thy blessed spirit bear a part,
And make up our defects with His sweet art.

  I got me flowers to strew thy way;
  I got me boughs of many a tree;
  But thou wast up by break of day,
  And brought'st thy sweets along with thee.

  The sunne arising in the East,—
  Though *he* give light, and th' East perfume;
  If they should offer to contest
  With thy arising, they presume.

  Can there be any day but this,
  Though many sunnes to shine endeavour?
  We count three hundred—but we miss;
  There is but one, and that one, ever.

GEORGE HERBERT.

ASSURANCES.

> "Who shall change our vile body, that it may be fashioned like unto His glorious body, according to the working whereby He is able even to subdue all things unto Himself." *Philippians,* iii. 21.

RED o'er the forest peers the setting sun,
    The line of yellow light dies fast away
That crowned the eastern copse: and chill and dun
    Falls on the moor the brief November day.

Now the tired hunter winds a parting note,
    And echo bids good-night from every glade;
Yet wait awhile and see the calm leaves float
    Each to his rest beneath their parent shade.

How like decaying life they seem to glide!
    And yet no second spring have they in store,
But where they fall, forgotten to abide
    Is all their portion and they ask no more.

Soon o'er their heads blithe April airs shall sing,
   A thousand wild-flowers round them shall unfold,
The green buds glisten in the dews of spring,
   And all the vernal rapture as of old.

Unconscious they in waste oblivion lie,
   In all the world of busy life around
No thought of them; in all the bounteous sky
   No drop, for them, of kindly influence found.

Man's portion is to die and rise again—
   Yet he complains, while these unmurmuring part
With their sweet lives, as pure from sin and stain
   As his when Eden held his virgin heart.

And haply half unblamed his murmuring voice
   Might sound in Heaven, were all his second life
Only the first renewed—the heathen's choice,
   A round of listless joys and weary strife.

For dreary were this earth, if earth were all,
   Though brightened oft by dear Affection's kiss;—
Who for the spangles wears the funeral pall?
   But catch a gleam beyond it, and 'tis bliss.

Heavy and dull this frame of limbs and heart,
  Whether slow creeping on cold earth, or borne
On lofty steed, or loftier prow, we dart
  O'er wave or field; yet breezes laugh to scorn

Our puny speed, and birds, and clouds in heaven,
  And fish, like living shafts that pierce the main,
And stars that shoot through freezing air at even—
  Who but would follow could he break his chain?

And thou shalt break it soon; the grovelling worm
  Shall find his wings, and soon as fast and free
As his transfigured Lord with lightning form
  And snowy vest—such grace He won for thee,

When from the grave He sprung at dawn of morn,
  And led through boundless air thy conquering road,
Leaving a glorious track, where saints, new-born,
  Might fearless follow to their blest abode.

But first, by many a stern and fiery blast
  .The world's rude furnace must thy blood refine,
And many a gale of keenest woe be passed,
  Till every pulse beat true to airs divine,

Till every limb obey the mounting soul,
  The mounting souls, the call by Jesus given—
He who the stormy heart can so control,
  The laggard body soon will waft to Heaven.

KEBLE.

ASCENDED INTO HEAVEN.

RISE—glorious Conqueror, rise,
Into Thy native skies,—
    Assume Thy right:
And where in many a fold
The clouds are backward rolled—
Pass through the gates of gold,
    And reign in light!

Victor o'er death and hell!
Cherubic legions swell
    The radiant train:
Praises all heaven inspire;
Each angel sweeps his lyre
And waves his wings of fire,
    Thou Lamb once slain!

Enter, Incarnate God!—
No feet, but Thine, have trod
    The serpent down:
Blow the full trumpets, blow!

Wider your portals throw!
Saviour—triumphant—go,
  And take Thy crown!

Yet—who are these behind,
In numbers more than mind
  Can count or say—
Clothed in immortal stoles,
Illumining the poles—
A galaxy of souls,
  In white array?

And then was heard afar
Star answering to star—
  Lo! these have come,
Followers of Him, who gave
His life, their lives to save;
And now their palms they wave
  Brought safely home.

Oh Lord! ascend Thy throne!
For Thou shalt rule alone
  Beside Thy Sire,
With the great Paraclete,
The Three in One complete—
Before whose awful feet
  All foes expire!

EGERTON BRYDGES.

LIFT UP YOUR HEARTS.

JOY of my life while left me here!
    And still my love!
How in Thy absence Thou dost steere
    Me from above!
    A life well led
    This truth commends,
    With quick or dead
    It never ends.

Stars are of mighty use: the night
    Is dark and long;
The road foul; and where one goes right,
    Six may go wrong.
    One twinkling ray,
    Shot o'er some cloud,
    May clear each way
    And guide a crowd.

God's saints are shining lights: who stays
    Here long must passe

O'er dark hills, swift streams, and steep ways
>	As smooth as glasse;
>	But these all night,
>	Like Candles, shed
>	Their beams, and light
>	Us into Bed.

They are indeed our Pillar-fires,
>	Seen as we go;
They are the Citie's shining spires
>	We travell to.
>	A sword-like gleame
>	Kept man from sin
>	First *Out;* this beame
>	Will guide him *In.*
>>	HENRY VAUGHN.

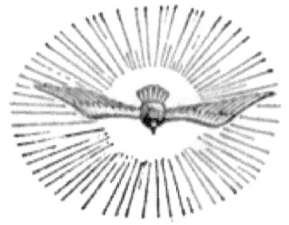

THE SAVIOUR'S GOING, GAIN.

"Nevertheless I tell you the truth; it is expedient for you that I go away; for if I go not away, the Comforter will not come unto you: but if I depart, I will send Him unto you." *St. John*, xvi. 7.

MY Saviour can it ever be
   That I should gain by losing Thee?
The watchful mother tarries nigh,
Though sleep have closed her infant's eye;
For should he wake and find her gone,
She knows she could not bear his moan.
But I am weaker than a child,
   And Thou art more than mother dear;
Without Thee Heaven were but a wild:
   How can I live without Thee here!

"'Tis good for you, that I should go,
"You lingering yet awhile below;"—
'Tis Thine own gracious promise, Lord!
Thy saints have proved the faithful word,

When Heaven's bright boundless avenue
Far opened on their eager view,
And homeward to Thy Father's throne,
   Still lessening, brightening on their sight,
Thy shadowy car went soaring on;
   They tracked Thee up th' abyss of light,

Thou bidd'st rejoice; they dare not mourn,
But to their home in gladness turn,
Their home and God's, that favoured place,
Where still He shines on Abraham's race,
In prayers and blessings there to wait
Like suppliants at their Monarch's gate,
Who bent with bounty rare to aid
   The splendors of His crowning day,
Keeps back awhile His largess, made
   More welcome for that brief delay:

In doubt they wait, but not unblest;
They doubt not of their Master's rest,
Nor of the gracious will of Heaven—
Who gave His Son, sure all was given—
But in ecstatic awe they muse
What course the genial stream may choose,
And far and wide their fancies rove,
   And to their height of wonder strain,
What secret miracle of love
   Should make their Saviour's going gain.

The days of hope and prayer are past,
The day of comfort dawns at last,
The everlasting gates again
Roll back, and lo! a royal train—
From the far depth of light once more
The floods of glory earthward pour;
They part like shower-drops in mid air,
   But ne'er so soft fell noontide shower,
Nor evening rainbow gleamed so fair
   To weary swains in parched bower.

Swiftly and straight each tongue of flame
Through cloud and breeze unwavering came,
And darted to its place of rest
On some meek brow of Jesus blest.
Nor fades it yet, that living gleam,
And still those lambent lightnings stream;
Where'er the Lord is, there are they;
   In every heart that gives them room,
They light His altar every day,
   Zeal to inflame and vice consume.

Soft as the plumes of Jesus' dove
They nurse the soul to heavenly love:
The struggling spark of good within,
Just smothered in the strife of sin,
They quicken to a timely glow,
The pure flame spreading high and low.

Said I, that prayer and hope are o'er?
   Nay, blessed Spirit! but by Thee
The Church's prayer finds wings to soar,
   The Church's hope finds eyes to see.

Then fainting soul arise and sing;
Mount, but be sober on the wing;
Mount up, for Heaven is won by prayer,
Be sober for thou art not there;
Till death the weary spirit free,
Thy God hath said, 'Tis good for thee
To walk by faith and not by sight:
   Take it on trust a little while;
Soon shalt thou read the mystery right
   In the full sunshine of His smile.

Or if thou yet more knowledge crave,
As thine own heart, that willing slave
To all that works thee woe or harm:
Should'st thou not need some mighty charm
To win thee to thy Saviour's side,
Though He had deigned with thee to bide?
The Spirit must stir the darkling deep,
   The Dove must settle on the Cross,
Else we should all sin on or sleep
   With Christ in sight, turning our gain to loss.

KEBLE.

THE LORD REIGNETH: LET THE EARTH REJOICE.

LORD God of might, in reverence lowly
    The hosts of heaven call Thee Holy;
      From cherubim and seraphim
    And angel phalanx far extending,
In fuller tones is still ascending
The Holy, Holy of their hymn.
    The fount of joy Thou art,
    That filleth every heart
      Ever, ever!
We too are Thine, and with them sing,
"Thou, Lord, and only Thou, art King."

Lord, there are bending now before Thee
The elders, with their crownéd glory,
    The first-born of the blesséd band;
There too earth's ransomed and forgiven,
Brought by the Saviour safe to heaven,
    In glad unnumbered myriads stand.
    Loud are the songs of praise
    Their mingled voices raise
      Ever, ever!

We too are Thine, and with them sing,
"Thou, Lord, and only Thou, art King."

They sing in sweet and sinless numbers
The wondrous love that never slumbers,
   And all the wisdom, power, and might,
The truth and faithfulness abiding,
And over all Thy works presiding;
   But they can scarcely praise aright:
      For all is never sung
      Even by seraph's tongue,
         Never, never!
We too are Thine, and with them sing,
"Thou, Lord, and only Thou, art King."

O come reveal Thyself more fully,
That we may learn to praise Thee truly;
   Make every heart a temple true,
Filled with Thy glory overflowing,
More of Thy love each morning showing,
   And waking praises loud and new:
      Here let Thy peace divine
      Upon Thy children shine
         Ever, ever!
That, glad or sad, we still may sing,
"Thou, Lord, and only Thou, art King."

THE GLORY OF GOD DID LIGHTEN IT.

HEAD of the Hosts in glory!
We joyfully adore Thee,—
　　Thy church on earth below,
Blending with those on high,—
Where through the azure sky
Thy saints in ecstacy,—
　　For ever glow!

Armies of God! in union
With us, through one communion,—
　　Pour forth sweet prayers:
Our souls in love's embrace,—
Around the Saviour's face,—
And ask His special grace
　　To soothe our cares.

Holy Apostles! beaming
With radiance brightly streaming
　　From diadems of power;

Call on the awful name,—
That we, through flood and flame
The gospel may proclaim
  In every hour!

Martyrs! whose mystic legions
March o'er yon heavenly regions
  In triumph round and round;
Wave—wave your banners—wave!
Your God—our Saviour, clave
For death itself a grave,—
  In hell profound!

Saints in fair circles, casting
Rich trophies everlasting
  At Jesu's piercéd feet,—
Amidst our rude alarms,
Stretch forth your conquering arms,
That we too, safe from harms,
  In Heaven may meet!

Angels—Archangels! glorious
Guards of the Church victorious!
  Worship the Lamb!
Crown Him with crowns of light,—
One of the Three by right,—
Love,—Majesty,—and Might,—
  The Great I AM.
EGERTON BRYDGES.

GO WORSHIP AT IMMANUEL'S FEET.

GO, worship at Immanuel's feet;
See in His face what wonders meet;
Earth is too narrow to express
His worth, His glory, or His grace!

The whole creation can afford
But some faint shadow of my Lord;
Nature, to make His beauties known,
Must mingle colours not her own.

Is He compared to Wine or Bread?
Dear Lord, our souls would that be fed:
That Flesh, that dying Blood of Thine,
Is Bread of Life, is heavenly Wine.

Is He a Tree? the world receives
Salvation from His healing leaves;
That righteous Branch, that fruitful bough,
Is David's root, and offspring too.

Is He a Rose? not Sharon yields
Such fragrancy in all her fields;
Or if the Lily He assume,
The valleys bless the rich perfume.

Is He a Vine? His heavenly root
Supplies the boughs with life and fruit;
O let a lasting union join
My soul the branch to Christ the Vine!

Is He the Head? Each member lives,
And owns the vital power He gives;
The Saints below and Saints above
Joined by His Spirit and His love.

Is He a Fountain? There I bathe,
And heal the plague of sin and death;
These waters all my soul renew,
And clense my spotted garments too.

Is He a Fire? He'll purge my dross;
But the true gold sustains no loss:
Like a Refiner shall He sit,
And tread the refuse with His feet.

Is He a Rock? How firm He proves!
The Rock of Ages never moves:

Yet the sweet streams, that from Him flow,
Attend us all the desert through.

Is He a Way?   He leads to God;
The path is drawn in lines of Blood;
There would I walk with zealous will
'Till I arrive at Zion's hill.

Is He a Door?   I'll enter in;
Behold the pastures large and green!
A paradise divinely fair;
None but the sheep have freedom there.

Is He designed a Corner Stone,
For men to build their Heaven upon?
I'll make Him my Foundation too;
Nor fear the plots of Hell below.

Is He a Temple?   I adore
The indwelling majesty and power;
And still to His Most Holy Place,
Whene'er I pray I turn my face.

Is He a Star?   He breaks the night,
Piercing the shades with dawning light;
I know His glories from afar,
I know the bright, the Morning Star!

Is He a Sun? His beams are grace,
His course a joy, and Righteousness:
Nations rejoice when He appears
To chase their clouds and dry their tears.

Oh! let me climb those higher skies
Where storms and darkness never rise!
There He displays His powers abroad,
And shines and reigns th' Incarnate God.

Nor earth, nor seas, nor sun, nor stars,
Nor Heaven His full resemblance bears;
His beauties we can never trace,
Till we behold Him face to face.

Isaac Watts, (1709.)

JESU REX ADMIRABILIS.

JESU! King most wonderful!
   Thou Conqueror renowned!
Thou Sweetness most ineffable!
   In whom all joys are found!

When once Thou visitest the heart,
   Then truth begins to shine;
Then earthly vanities depart;
   Then kindles love divine.

O Jesu! Light of all below!
   Thou Fount of life and fire!
Surpassing all the joys we know,
   All that we can desire:

May every heart confess Thy name
   And ever Thee adore;
And seeking Thee, itself inflame
   To seek Thee more and more.

Thee may our tongues for ever bless;
  Thee may we love alone;
And ever in our lives express
  The image of Thine own.

CASWALL.

JESU DULCIS MEMORIA.

JESU! the very thought of Thee
    With sweetness fills my breast;
But sweeter far Thy face to see,
    And in Thy presence rest.

Nor voice can sing, nor heart can frame,
    Nor can the memory find,
A sweeter sound than Thy blest name,
    O Saviour of mankind!

O hope of every contrite heart,
    O joy of all the meek,
To those who fall, how kind Thou art!
    How good to those who seek!

But what to those who find? ah! this
    Nor tongue nor pen can show:
The love of Jesus, what it is,
    None but His loved ones know.

Jesu! our only joy be Thou,
    As Thou our prize will be;
Jesu! be Thou our glory now,
    And through eternity.

                    CASWALL.

JESU DECUS ANGELICUM.

JESU! Thou the beauty art
  Of angel worlds above;
Thy name is music to the heart,
  Enchanting it with love.

Celestial sweetness unalloyed!
  Who eat Thee hunger still;
Who drink of Thee still feel a void,
  Which naught but Thou can fill.

O my sweet Jesus! hear the sighs
  Which unto Thee I send;
To Thee mine inmost spirit cries,
  My being's hope and end!

Stay with us, Lord, and with Thy light
  Illume the soul's abyss;
Scatter the darkness of our night,
  And fill the world with bliss.

O Jesu! spotless Virgin flower!
  Our life and joy! to Thee
Be praise, beatitude, and power,
  Through all eternity.
CASWALL.

CROWNED WITH GLORY AND HONOUR.

TO Him who for our sins was slain,
To Him, for all His dying pain,
    Sing we Hallelujah!
To Him, the Lamb our sacrifice,
Who gave His soul our ransom price,
    Sing we Hallelujah!

To Him that died that we might die
To sin, and live with Him on high,
    Sing we Hallelujah!
To Him who rose that we might rise
And reign with Him beyond the skies
    Sing we Hallelujah!

To Him who now for us doth plead,
And helpeth us in all our need,
    Sing we Hallelujah!
To Him who doth prepare on high
Our home in immortality
    Sing we Hallelujah!

To Him be glory evermore;
Ye heavenly hosts, your Lord adore;
  Sing ye Hallelujah!
To Father, Son, and Holy Ghost,
One God most high, our joy and boast,
  Sing we Hallelujah!

WHEN JESUS CAME TO EARTH OF OLD.

WHEN Jesus came to earth of old,
    He came in weakness and in woe;
He wore no form of angel mould,
    But took our nature poor and low.

But when He cometh back once more,
    There shall be set the Great White Throne,
And earth and heaven shall flee before
    The face of Him that sits thereon.

O Son of God, in glory crowned,
    The Judge ordained of quick and dead;
O Son of man, so pitying found
    For all the tears Thy people shed;—

Be with us in this darkened place,
    This weary, restless, dangerous night;

And teach, O teach us by Thy grace
    To struggle onward into light.

And since in God's recording book
    Our sins are written every one,—
The crime, the wrath, the wandering look,
    The good we knew, and left undone;—

Lord, ere the last dread trumpet sound,
    And ere before Thy face we stand,
Look Thou on each accusing word,
    And blot it with Thy bleeding hand.

And by the love that brought Thee here,
    And by the Cross and by the Grave,
Give perfect love for conscious fear,
    And in the Day of Judgment save.

And lead us on, while here we stay,
    And make us love our earthly home;
Till from our hearts we learn to say,
    "Even so Lord Jesus, quickly come."
                        C. F. ALEXANDER.

WHILST THE CARELESS WORLD IS SLEEPING.

WHILST the careless world is sleeping,
Blest the servants who are keeping
   Watch, according to His Word,
   For the coming of their Lord.

At His table He will place them,
With His royal banquet grace them,
   Banquet that shall never cloy;
   Bread of life and wine of joy.

Heard ye not your Master's warning?
He will come before the morning,
   Unexpected, undescried;
   Watch ye for Him open-eyed.

Teach us so to watch, Lord Jesus;
From the sleep of sin release us:
   Swift to hear Thee let us be,
   Meet to enter in with Thee.

God who with all good provides us,
God who made, who saved, who guides us,
  Praise we with the heavenly host,
  Father, Son, and Holy Ghost.

HOLY AND REVEREND IS HIS NAME.

HOSANNA to the living Lord!
Hosanna to the incarnate Word,
To Christ, Creator, Saviour, King,
Let earth, let heaven, Hosanna sing,
 Hosanna, Lord, Hosanna in the highest!

O Saviour, with protecting care
Return to this Thy house of Prayer:
Where we Thy parting promise claim,
Assembled in Thy sacred name:
 Hosanna, Lord, Hosanna in the highest!

But, chiefest, in our cleansèd breast,
Eternal, bid Thy Spirit rest,
And make our secret soul to be
A temple pure, and worthy Thee:
 Hosanna, Lord, Hosanna in the highest!

So, in the last and dreadful day,
When earth and heaven shall melt away,
Thy flock, redeemed from sinful stain,
Shall swell the sound of praise again:
   Hosanna, Lord, Hosanna in the highest!

YE DO SHOW THE LORD'S DEATH UNTIL HE COME.

BY Christ redeemed, in Christ restored,
We keep the memory adored,
And show the death of our dear Lord,
    Until He come!

His body broken in our stead,
Is here, in this memorial bread;
And so our feeble love is fed,
    Until He come!

His fearful drops of agony,
His life-blood shed for us we see;
The wine shall tell the mystery,
    Until He come!

And thus that dark betrayal-night,
With the last Advent we unite;
The shame! the glory! by this Rite,
    Until He come!

Until the trump of God be heard,
Until the ancient graves be stirred,
And with the great commanding word,
    The Lord shall come!

O blessed Hope! with this elate
Let not our hearts be desolate,
But strong in faith, in patience wait,
    Until He come!

THY KINGDOM COME.

LORD! come away!
    Why dost Thou stay?
    Thy road is ready; and Thy paths
      made straight
With longing expectation wait
The consecration of Thy beauteous feet!
Ride on triumphantly! Behold, we lay
    Our lusts and proud wills in Thy way!

Hosanna! Welcome to our hearts! Lord, here
Thou hast a temple too; and full as dear
As that of Sion, and as full of sin:
Nothing but thieves and robbers dwell therein:
Enter, and chase them forth, and cleanse the
      floor!
Crucify them, that they may never more
    Profane that holy place
      Where Thou hast chose to set Thy face!
      And then, if our stiff tongues shall be

Mute in the praises of Thy Deity,
   The stones out of the temple wall
     Shall cry aloud, and call
Hosanna! and Thy glorious footsteps greet!
                              Amen.
     BISHOP JEREMY TAYLOR, (1655.)

WATCHING AND WAITING.

"And at midnight there was a cry made, Behold, the Bridegroom cometh; go ye out to meet Him." *Matt.* xxv.

WAKE, ye holy maidens, fearing
To slumber out your Lord's appearing;
Hear ye the watchful herald's cry:
Wake, Jerusalem, midnight tolleth;
Hark, how His chariot onward rolleth!
List, virgins rise, He draweth nigh:
Rise up; with willing feet
Go out, the Bridegroom meet!
Alleluia!
Bear through the night
Your well-trimmed light;
Speed forth to join the marriage rite.

Zion hears the herald's singing;
Her heart of hearts with joy is springing.
She starteth up, she hastes away!

Onward her Bridegroom cometh glorious,
In grace arrayed, by truth victorious;
   Her grief is joy, her night is day.
Come, worthy Champion,
O Christ, the Almighty Son:
        Hosanna!
We glide along
In pomp of song,
In haste to join the marriage throng.

Hymns of praise to Thee be given,
By men on earth and saints in heaven.
   With harp, and lute, and psaltery:
Gates of pearl do guard Thy treasure,
We stand before them keeping measure,
   In bursts of choral melody
No vision ever bore,
No ear hath heard before:
        Allelulia!
Yea, now will we
With holy glee
Renew this strain eternally.   Amen.

DIES IRÆ, DIES ILLA.

AY of anger, that dread Day
Shall the Sign in Heaven display,
And the Earth in ashes lay.

O what trembling shall appear,
When His coming shall be near,
Who shall all things strictly clear!

When the trumpet shall command
Through the tombs of every land
All before the Throne to stand;

Death shall shrink and nature quake,
When all creatures shall awake,
Answer to their God to make.

See the Book divinely penn'd,
In which all is found contain'd
Whence the world shall be arraign'd!

When the Judge is on His Throne,
All that's hidden shall be shown,
Nought unpunished or unknown!

What shall I before Him say?
How shall I be safe that day,
When the righteous scarcely may?

King of awful majesty,
Saving sinners graciously,
Fount of mercy, save Thou me!

Leave me not my Saviour, one
For whose soul Thy course was run,
Lest I be that day undone.

Thou didst toil my soul to gain,
Didst redeem me with Thy pain;
Be such labour not in vain!

Thou just Judge of wrath severe,
Grant my sins remission here,
Ere Thy reckoning day appear.

My transgressions grevious are;
Scarce look up for shame I dare;
Lord, Thy guilty suppliant spare!

Thou didst heal the sinner's grief,
And didst hear the dying thief:
Even I may hope relief.

All unworthy is my prayer;
Make my soul Thy mercy's care,
And from fire eternal spare.

Place me with Thy sheep, that band
Who shall separated stand
From the goats, at Thy right hand!

When Thy voice in wrath shall say,
Cursèd one, depart away!
Call me with the blest, I pray!

Lord Thine ear in mercy bow!
Broken is my heart and low:
Guard of my last end be Thou!

In that day, that mournful day,
When to judgment wakes our clay,
Show me mercy, Lord, I pray!

    HENRY ALFORD, (1845.)

THE DAY OF HIS COMING.

WHEN God of old came down from Heaven,
  In power and wrath He came;
Before His feet the clouds were riven,
  Half darkness and half flame.

Around the trembling mountain's base
  The prostrate people lay;
A day of wrath and not of grace;
  A dim and dreadful day.

But when He came the second time,
  He came in power and love;
Softer than gale at morning prime,
  Hovered His holy Dove.

The fires that rushed on Sinai down
  In sudden torrents dread,
Now gently light, a glorious crown,
  On every sainted head.

Like arrows went those lightnings forth,
    Winged with the sinner's doom:
But these, like tongues, o'er all the earth,
    Proclaiming life to come.

And as on Israel's awe-struck ear
    The voice exceeding loud,
The trump, that angels quake to hear,
    Thrilled from the deep dark cloud;

So when the spirit of our God
    Came down, His flock to find,
A voice from heaven was heard abroad,
    A rushing mighty wind.

Nor doth the outward ear alone
    At that high warning start;
Conscience gives back th' appalling tone;
    'Tis echoed from the heart.

It fills the Church of God, it fills
    The sinful world around;
Only in stubborn hearts and wills
    No place for it is found.

To other strains our souls are set;
    A giddy whirl of sin

Fills ear and brain, and will not let
   Heaven's harmonies come in.

Come Lord, come Wisdom, Love, and
   Power;
   Open our ears to hear;
Let us not miss the accepted hour;
   Save, Lord, by love or fear!

JOHN KEBLE, (1827.)

IN THE CLOUDS OF HEAVEN.

LO! He comes with clouds descending,
    Once for favor'd sinners slain;
    Thousand—thousand saints attending,
Swell the triumph of His train:
Alleluia! Alleluia!
Jesus Christ shall ever reign!

See the universe in motion,
    Sinking in her funeral pyre,—
Earth dissolving, and the ocean
    Vanishing in final fire:—
    Hark, the trumpet! Hark the trumpet!
    Loud proclaims the Day of Ire!

Graves have yawned in countless numbers,—
    From the dust the dead arise:
Millions, out of silent slumbers,
    Wake in overwhelmed surprise;

Where creation,—where creation,
  Wrecked and torn in ruin lies!

See the Judge our nature wearing,
  Pure, ineffable, divine;—
See the great Archangel bearing
  High in Heaven the mystic sign:
  Cross of Glory! Cross of Glory!
  Christ be in that moment mine!

Every eye shall then behold Him
  Robed in awful majesty:
Those that set at nought, and sold Him,
  Pierced and nailed Him to a tree,—
  Deeply wailing,—Deeply wailing,
  Shall the true Messiah see!

Lo! the last long separation!
  As the clearing clouds divide;
And one dread adjudication
  Sends each soul to either side!
  Lord of mercy! Lord of mercy!
  How shall I that day abide!

Oh! may Thine own Bride and Spirit
  Then avert a dreadful doom,—
And we summon to inherit
  An eternal blissful home;—

8

Ah! come quickly! Ah! come quickly,
Let Thy second Advent come!

Yea, Amen! Let all adore Thee
  On Thine amaranthine throne!
Saviour! take the power and glory,
  Claim the kingdom for thine own!
Men and angels: Men and angels,
Kneel and bow to Thee alone!

EGERTON BRYDGES.

WHO IS THIS THAT COMETH LEAN-ING ON HER BELOVED?

I JOURNEY through a desert drear and wild,
    Yet is my heart by such sweet thoughts beguiled
Of Him on whom I lean, my strength, my stay,
That I forget the sorrows of the way.

Thoughts of His love, the root of every grace
Which finds in this poor heart a dwelling place,
The sunshine of my soul, than day more bright,
And my calm pillow of repose by night.

Thoughts of His sojourn in this vale of tears:—
The tale of love unfolded in those years,
Of sinless suffering and patient grace,
I love again and yet again to trace.

Thoughts of His glory: on the Cross I gaze,
And there behold its sad yet healing rays;

Beacon of hope, which lifted up on high
Illumed with heavenly light the tear-dimmed eye.

Thoughts of His coming: for that joyful day
In patient hope I watch and wait and pray;
The dawn draws nigh, the midnight shadows flee;
O what a sunrise will that advent be!

Thus while I journey on my Lord to meet,
My thoughts and meditations are so sweet
Of Him on whom I lean, my strength, my stay,
That I forget the sorrows of the way.

STRENGTHENED WITH MIGHT BY HIS SPIRIT IN THE INNER MAN.

COME to our poor nature's might,
With Thy blessèd inward light,
Holy Ghost the Infinite.
  Comforter divine:
We are sinful; cleanse us, Lord;
Sick and faint; Thy strength afford:
Lost, until by Thee restored,
  Comforter divine.

Orphan are our souls, and poor;
Give us from Thy heavenly store
Faith, love, joy, for evermore,
  Comforter divine:
Like the dew, Thy peace distil;
Guide, subdue our wayward will,
Things of Christ unfolding still.
  Comforter divine.

Gentle, awful, holy Guest,
Make Thy temple in each breast
Shrine of purity confessed,
  Comforter divine:
In us, for us, intercede,
And with voiceless groanings plead
Our unutterable need,
  Comforter divine.

In us, "Abba, Father," cry,
Earnest of our bliss on high,
Seal of immortality,
  Comforter divine:
Search for us the depths of God;
Bear us up the starry road
To the height of Thine abode,
  Comforter divine.

THROUGH HIM WE HAVE ACCESS BY ONE SPIRIT UNTO THE FATHER.

HOLY Spirit, given
  For our guide to heaven,
    Sent by love divine;
  With Thy peace consoling,
Every ill controlling,
  On our darkness shine!
Faith and hope and love increasing,
Fill our hearts with joy unceasing.

Lord, of life the Giver,
Dwell with us forever:
  Heavenly life inspire:
All within renewing,
With Thy grace enduing
  Heart, mind, thought, desire!
Fount of life forever flowing,
Grace and peace on us bestowing.

Fill our meditation
With Thine inspiration:

Graft us in Thy word:
So may we possessing
Thine all-fruitful blessing,
   Glorify our Lord,
Follow Him with faith unfeignéd,
Till we have His rest attainéd.

Only through His merit
We Thine aid inherit:
   In His Name we plead:
Never let us grieve Thee,
But with joy receive Thee,
   Fulness of our need:
In our wealth, and in affliction,
Crown us with Thy benediction.   Amen.

IT IS THE SPIRIT THAT QUICKENETH.

HOLY Spirit, Lord of Light,
From Thy clear celestial height
  Thy pure beaming radiance give:
Come, Thou Father of the poor,
Come, with treasures that endure,
  Come, Thou Light of all that live.

Thou, of all consolers best,
Visiting the troubled breast,
  Dost refreshing peace bestow;
Thou in toil and comfort sweet,
Cooling breath in noontide heat,
  Solace in the hour of woe.

Light most blissful, Light divine,
Visit Thou these hearts of Thine,
  And our inmost being fill!
If Thou take Thy grace away,
Nothing pure in man will stay;
  All his good is turned to ill.

Heal our wounds; our strength renew;
On our dryness pour Thy dew;
   Wash the stains of guilt away;
Bend the stubborn heart and will;
Kindle what is cold and chill;
   Guide the steps that go astray.

Thou, on all who evermore
Thee confess and Thee adore,
   In Thy seven-fold gifts descend:
Give them comfort when they die;
Give them their reward on high;
   Give them joys which never end. Amen.

THOU WHOSE ALMIGHTY WORD.

THOU Whose almighty word
Chaos and darkness heard,
   And took their flight!
Hear us we humbly pray,
And where the Gospel day
Sheds not its glorious ray,
   Let there be Light!

Thou Who didst come to bring
On Thy redeeming wing
   Healing and light,—
Health to the sick in mind,
Sight to the inly blind,
O, now to all mankind,
   Let there be Light.

Spirit of truth and love,
Life-giving, holy Dove,
   Speed forth Thy flight!
Move on the water's face,

Spreading the beams of grace,
And in earth's darkest place
   Let there be Light!

Blessed and holy Three,
Glorious Trinity,
   Wisdom, Love, Might!
Boundless as ocean's tide,
Rolling in fullest pride,
Through the world, far and wide,
   Let there be Light!

JOHN MARRIOTT.

WALK IN THE LIGHT.

WALK in the light, and thou shalt know
  That fellowship of love
His spirit only can bestow,
  Who reigns in light above.
Walk in the light, and sin abhorred
  Shall ne'er defile again;
The blood of Jesus Christ the Lord
  Shall cleanse from every stain.

Walk in the light and thou shalt find
  Thy heart made truly His
Who dwells in cloudless light enshrined;
  With whom no darkness is.
Walk in the light, and thou shalt own
  Thy mists have passed away,
Because in thee that light hath shone
  Which grows to perfect day.

Walk in the light, and e'en the tomb
  No fearful shade shall mar;

Glory shall chase away its gloom,
  For Christ hath conquered there.
Walk in the light, and there shall be
  A path, if thorny, bright;
For God by grace shall dwell in thee,
  And God Himself is light.

              BERNARD BARTON.

VENI CREATOR SPIRITUS.

HOLY Spirit, gently come,
  Raise us from our fallen state,
Fix Thy everlasting home
  In the hearts Thou didst create,
    Gift of God most High!
Visit every troubled breast:
Light and life and love supply;
Give our spirits perfect rest.

Heavenly unction from above,
Comforter of weary saints,
Fountain, Life, and Fire of Love,
Hear and answer our complaints!
    Thee we humbly pray,
Finger of the Living God,
Now Thy seven-fold grace display,
Shed our Saviour's love abroad!

Now Thy quickening influence bring,
On our spirits sweetly move;

Open every mouth to sing
Jesus' everlasting love!
   Lighten every heart;
Drive our enemies away;
Joy and peace to us impart:
Lead us in the heavenly way!

Take the things of Christ and show
What our Lord for us hath done;
May we God the Father know
Only in and through the Son;
   Nothing will we fear,
Though to wilds and deserts driven,
While we feel Thy presence near,
Witnessing our sins forgiven.

Glory be to God alone,
God whose hand created all!
Glory be to God the Son,
Who redeem'd us from our fall!
   To the Holy Ghost
Equal praise and glory be,
When the course of time is lost,
Lost in wide eternity!

WILLIAM HAMMOND, (1745.)

SWEET IS THE SPIRIT'S STRAIN.

SWEET is the Spirit's strain;
  Breathed by soft pleadings inly heard,
  By all the heart's deep fountains stirred,
By conscience, and the written Word;
  Come, wanderers, home again!

  The Bride repeats the call;
By high thanksgiving, lowly prayer,
By days of rest, and fostering care,
By holy rites, that all may share;
  She whispers, Come! to all.

  Let him who hears say, Come!
If thou hast been sin's wretched slave;
If thou art risen from that grave;
Thy sleeping brethren seek to save,
  And call the wanderers home.

And let all come, who thirst!
Freely for every child of woe
The streams of living waters flow;
And whosoever will may go
  Where healing fountains burst.

There drink and be at rest;
On Him who died for thee believe;
The Spirit's quickening grace receive;
No more the God who seeks thee grieve;
  Be holy and be blest!

JOSEPH ANSTICE, (1836.)

HE HATH NOT LEFT HIMSELF WITHOUT WITNESS.

THERE is a book, who runs may read,
  Which heavenly truth imparts;
And all the lore its scholars need,
  Pure eyes and Christian hearts.

The works of God, above, below,
  Within us and around,
Are pages in that book, to show
  How God Himself is found.

The glorious sky embracing all,
  Is like the Maker's love,
Wherewith encompassed, great and small
  In peace and order move.

The moon above, the Church below,
  A wondrous race they run;
But all their radiance, all their glow,
  Each borrows of its sun.

The Saviour lends the light and heat
   That crowns His holy will;
The saints, like stars, around His seat
   Perform their courses still.

The saints above are stars in Heaven;
   What are the saints on earth?
Like trees they stand, whom God has given,
   Our Eden's happy birth.

Faith is their fix'd unswerving root,
   Hope their unfading flower;
Fair deeds of charity their fruit,
   The glory of their bower.

The dew of Heaven is like Thy grace;
   It steals in silence down;
But, where it lights, the favoured place
   By richest fruits is known.

One name, above all glorious names,
   With its ten thousand tongues
The everlasting sea proclaims,
   Echoing angelic songs.

The raging fire, the roaring wind,
   The boundless power display:

But in the gentler breeze we find
   Thy spirit's viewless way.

Two worlds are ours; 'tis only sin
   Forbids us to descry,
The mystic heaven and earth within,
   Plain as the sea and sky.

Thou who hast given us eyes to see
   And love this sight so fair,
Give us a heart to find out Thee,
   And read Thee everywhere.

                    KEBLE, (1827.)

THE KINGDOM OF GOD.

I SAY to thee, do thou repeat
To the first man thou mayest meet
In lane, highway, or open street—

That he, and we, and all men, move
Under a canopy of love,
As broad as the blue sky above:

That doubt and trouble, fear and pain
And anguish, all are shadows vain;
That death itself shall not remain:

That weary deserts we may tread,
A dreary labyrinth may thread,
Through dark ways underground be led:

Yet, if we will one Guide obey,
The dreariest path, the darkest way,
Shall issue out in heavenly day.

And we on diverse shores now cast,
Shall meet, our perilous voyage past,
All in our Father's house at last.

And ere thou leave him, say thou this,
Yet one word more: they only miss
The winning of that final bliss—

Who will not count it true that Love,
Blessing, not cursing, rules above,
And that in it we live and move.

And one thing further make him know—
That to believe these things are so,
This firm faith never to forego—

Despite of all which seems at strife
With blessing, all with curses rife—
That this *is* blessing, this *is* life.

R. C. Trench.

THE SURE COVENANT.

"For this is as the waters of Noah unto Me; for as I have sworn the waters shall no more go over the earth, so have I sworn that I would not be wroth with thee."

LET the storms ply their deep and threat'-
    ning bass,
    The bow of promise shall the
    shades illume,
Brightly descried in Faith's eternal glass,
    E'en like an Angel's many coloured plume
    Waving in tempest—pledge that in her bloom
Nature, emerging from the stormy mass,
Will keep her time and order,—Let them pass
    The wicked and their plottings: 'mid the gloom,
    The Church surveys her covenant sign, and smiles:
    And 'neath her solemn rainbow's dripping arch,
    A mystic wing spread o'er her daring march,

She goes forth, on her heavenly work the whiles,
 Though weeping, sure that One in joy shall bring,
 Her and her sheaves at harvest-moon to sing.

From the Cathedral.

I AM WITH YOU ALWAYS.

A THOUSAND years have fleeted;
    And, Saviour! still we see
Thy deed of love repeated
    On all who come to Thee.
As he who sat benighted,
    Afflicted, poor, and blind;
So now, (Thy word is plighted,)
    Joy, light, and peace I find.

Dark gloom my spirit filling,
    Beside the way I sat;
Desire my heart was thrilling;
    But anguish more than that.
To me no ray was granted,
    Although I heard the psalms,
The faithful sweetly chanted,
    And felt the waving palms.

With grief my heart was aching;
    O'erwhelming were my woes,

Till, heaven-born courage taking,
  To Thee my cry arose:
"O David's Son, relieve me,
  "My bitter anguish quell;
"Thy promised succour give me,
  "And this dark night dispel!"

With tears that fast were flowing,
  I sought Thee through the crowd,
My heart more tender growing,
  Until I wept aloud:
Oh! then my grief diminished;
  For then they cried to me,
"Blind man, thy woe is finished;
  "Arise, He calleth thee!"

I came with steps that faltered;
  Thy course I felt Thee check;
Then straight my mind was altered,
  And bowed my stubborn neck:
Thou saidst, "What art thou seeking?"
  "Oh Lord! that I might see!"
Oh! then I heard Thee speaking;
  "Believe, and it shall be."

Our hope, Lord, faileth never,
  When Thou Thy word dost plight:

My fears then ceased forever,
　And all my soul was light.
Thou gavest me Thy blessing;
　From former guilt set free,
Now heavenly joy possessing,
　O Lord! I follow Thee!

FRANCES ELIZABETH COX, (1841.)
From Fouque.

PASTOR ANIMARUM.

COME wandering sheep, O come!
   I'll bind thee to my breast;
I'll bear thee to thy home,
   And lay thee down to rest.

I saw thee stray forlorn,
   And heard the faintly cry,
And on the tree of scorn
   For thee I deigned to die—
   What greater proof could I
Give,—than to seek the tomb?
Come, wandering sheep, O come!

I shield thee from alarms,
   And wilt thou not be blest?
I bear thee in my arms;
   Thou, bear Me in thy breast!
   O, this is love—come, rest—
This is a blissful doom.
Come, wandering sheep, O come!

Lyra Catholica.

IN MY FATHER'S HOUSE.

LONG did I toil, and knew no earthly rest;
  Far did I rove, and found no certain home;
At last I sought them in His sheltering breast,
  Who opes His arms, and bids the weary come:
With Him I found a home, a rest divine;
And I since then am His, and He is mine.

Yes! He is mine! and nought of earthly things,
  Not all the charms of pleasure, wealth, or power,
The fame of heroes, or the pomp of kings,
  Could tempt me to forego His love an hour.
Go, worthless world, I cry, with all that's thine!
Go, I my Saviour's am, and He is mine!

The good I have is from His stores supplied;
  The ill is only what He deems the best;
He for my Friend, I'm rich with nought beside;
  And poor without Him, though of all possest;
Changes may come; I take, or I resign;
Content, while I am His, and He is mine.

Whate'er may change, in Him no change is seen;
  A glorious Sun, that wanes not nor declines;
Above the clouds and storms He walks serene,
  And sweetly on his people's darkness shines:
All may depart; I fret not nor repine,
While I my Saviour's am, while He is mine.

He stays me falling, lifts me up when down,
  Reclaims me wandering, guards from every foe;
Plants on my worthless brow the victor's crown;
  Which, in return, before His feet I throw,
Grieved that I cannot better grace His shrine,
Who deigns to own me His, as He is mine.

While here, alas! I know but half His love,
  But half discern Him, and but half adore;

But when I meet Him in the realms above,
  I hope to love Him better, praise Him more,
And feel, and tell, amid the choir Divine,
How fully I am His, and He is mine.
          HENRY FRANCIS LYTE, (1833.)

THE HOLY SCRIPTURES.

I.

 BOOK! infinite sweetness! let my heart
    Suck every letter; and a honey gain,
Precious for every grief in any part,
    To clear the breast, to mollify all pain.

Thou art all health; health thriving till it make
    A full eternity. Thou art a mass
Of strange delights, where we may wish and take.
    *   *   *   *   *

      *   * this is the well
    That washes what it shears. Who can endear
    Thy praise too much? Thou art Heav'n's lieger here,
Working against the states of Death and Hell.

II.

Oh that I knew how all thy lights combine,
    And the configuration of their glory!
Seeing not only how each verse doth shine,
    But all the constellations of the story.

This verse marks that, and both do make a motion
    Unto a third, that ten leaves off doth lie.
Then, as dispersed herbs do watch a potion,
    These three make up some Christian's destiny.

Such are thy secrets, which my life makes good,
    And comments on thee. For in every thing
    Thy words do find me out, and parallels bring,
And in another make me understood.

Stars are poor books, and oftentimes do miss:
This book of stars lights to eternal bliss.

GEORGE HERBERT.

HOLY BAPTISM.

IN token that thou shalt not fear
    Christ crucified to own,
We print the cross upon thee here,
    And stamp thee His alone.

In token that thou shalt not blush
    We glory in His name,
We blazon here upon thy front
    His glory and His shame.

In token that thou shalt not fail
    Christ's quarrel to maintain,
But 'neath His banner manfully
    Firm at thy post remain;

In token that thou too shalt tread
    The path He travelled by,
Endure the cross, despise the shame,
    And sit thee down on high;

Thus, outwardly and visibly,
  We seal thee for His own;
And may the brow that wears His cross
  Hereafter share His crown!

    HENRY ALFORD, (1845.)

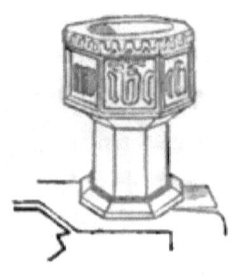

CONFIRMATION PRAYER.

THINE for ever! God of love,
Hear us from Thy throne above;
Thine forever may we be,
Here and in eternity!

Thine for ever! Lord of life,
Shield us through our earthly strife;
Thou, the Life, the Truth, the Way,
Guide us to the realms of day.

Thine for ever! O how blest
They who find in Thee their rest;
Saviour, Guardian, heavenly Friend,
O defend us to the end.

Thine for ever! Saviour keep
These Thy frail and trembling sheep;
Safe alone beneath Thy care
Let us all Thy goodness share.

Thine for ever! Thou our Guide,
All our wants by Thee supplied,
All our sins by Thee forgiven,
Led by Thee from earth to heaven!
                              Amen.

EUCHARIST.

HE cometh, on yon hallowed Board
    The ready Feast doth duly show,
Where wait the chalice and the bread,
    Like jems within their veil of snow.

He cometh, as He came of old,
    Suddenly to His Father's shrine,
Into the hearts he died to make
    Meet temples for His grace Divine.

He cometh, as the Bridegroom comes,
    Unto the feast Himself has spread;
His flesh and blood the heavenly food
    Wherewith the wedding guests are fed.

He cometh—gentle as the dew,
    And sweet as drops of honey clear,
And good as God's own manna shower,
    To longing souls that meet Him here.

He cometh—let not one withdraw,
  Nor fear to bring repented sin;
There's blood to wash, there's bread to feed,
  And Christ Himself to enter in.

He cometh—praises in the Church,
  And Hymns of praise in Heaven above,
And in our hearts repentant faith,
  And love that springs to meet His love.

C. F. ALEXANDER.

II.

O Jesu, bruised and wounded more
  Than bursted grape, or bread of wheat;
The Life of Life within our souls,
  The cup of our salvation sweet;

We come to shew Thy dying hour,
  Thy streaming vein, Thy broken flesh;
And still the blood is warm to save,
  And still the fragrant wounds are fresh.

O heart, that with a double tide
  Of blood and water, maketh pure;
O flesh, once offered on the Cross,
  The gift that makes our pardon sure:

Let never more our sinful souls
   The anguish of Thy cross renew;
Nor forge again the cruel nails
   That pierced Thy victim Body through.

Come Bread of Heaven, to feed our souls,
   And with Thee Jesu, enter in;
Come, Wine of God, and as we drink
   His precious blood, wash out our sin.

C. F. ALEXANDER.

EATING AND DRINKING WITH CHRIST.

HERE I sink before Thee lowly,
Filled with gladness deep and holy,
As with trembling awe and wonder
On Thy mighty work I ponder,
  On this banquet's mystery,
  On the depths we cannot see;
  Far beyond all mortal sight
  Lie the secrets of Thy might.

Sun, who all my life dost brighten,
Light who dost my soul enlighten,
Joy, the sweetest man e'er knoweth,
Fount, whence all my being floweth,
  Humbly draw I near to Thee;
  Grant that I may worthily
  Take this blessèd heavenly food,
  To Thy praise, and to my good.

Jesus, Bread of Life from heaven,
Never be Thou vainly given,

Nor I to my hurt invited;
Be Thy love with love requited;
  Let me learn its depths indeed,
  While on Thee my soul doth feed;
  Let me, here so richly blest,
  Be hereafter too Thy guest.

THE HOLY COMMUNION.

ELCOME sweet, sacred feast!
O welcome life!
Dead I was, and deep in trouble;
But grace and blessing came with Thee so rife,
That they have quicken'd even drie stubble.
Thus soules their bodies animate,
And thus at first when things were rude,
Dark, void, and crude,
They by Thy Word their beauty had and date;
All were by Thee,
And still must be;
Nothing that is, or lives,
But hath His Quickenings, and reprieves,
As Thy hand opes or shuts;
Healings and cuts,
Darkness, and day-light, life, and death
Are but meer leaves turn'd by Thy breath.
Spirits without Thee die,
And blackness sits
On the divinest wits,

As on the sun eclipses lie.
But that great darkness at Thy death,
When the veyl broke with Thy last breath,
      Did make us see
      The way to Thee;
And now by these sure, sacred ties,
      After Thy blood
      Our sov'rain good,
      Had clear'd our eies,
      And given us sight;
Thou dost unto Thyself betroth
    Our souls and bodies both
    In everlasting light.

Was't not enough that Thou had'st pay'd the
    price,
    And given us eies,
When we had none, but thou must also take
    Us by the hand,
    And keep us still awake,
      When we would sleep,
      Or from Thee creep,
Who without Thee cannot stand?

    Was't not enough to lose Thy breath
    And blood by an accursed death,
      But Thou must also leave
      To us, that did bereave

Thee of them both, these seals, the means
    That should both cleanse
      And keep us so,
   Who wrought Thy wo?
O Rose of *Sharon!* O the Lily
    Of the Valley!
How art thou now, thy flock to keep,
Become both *food*, and *Shepheard* to Thy sheep!

        HENRY VAUGHN, (1650.)

REST UNTO YOUR SOULS.

LORD what a change within us one short hour
    Spent in Thy presence will prevail to make—
What heavy burdens from our bosoms take,
What parchéd grounds refresh, as with a shower!
We kneel, and all around us seems to lower;
We rise, and all, the distant and the near,
Stands forth in sunny outline, brave and clear;
We kneel how weak, we rise how full of power!
Why, therefore, should we do ourselves this wrong,
Or others—that we are not always strong!
That we are ever overborne with care;
That we should ever weak or heartless be,
Anxious or troubled, when with us in prayer,
And joy, and strength, and courage, are with Thee?

R. C. TRENCH.

MINISTERING ANGELS.

They are evermore around us, though unseen to mortal sight,
In the golden hour of sunshine, and in sorrow's starless night,
Deepening earth's most sacred pleasures, with the peace of sins forgiven,
Whispering to the lonely mourner of the painless joys of Heaven.

Lovingly they come to help us, when our faith is cold and weak,
Guiding us along the pathway to the blessed Home we seek;
In our hearts we hear their voices, breathing sympathy and love,
Echoes of the spirit-language in the sinless world above.

They are with us in the conflict, with their words of hope and cheer,

When the foe of our salvation and his armèd hosts draw near;
And a greater One is with us, and we shrink not from the strife,
While the Lord of angels leads us on the battle-field of life.

Seldom do we think upon them, seldom we believe them nigh,—
Like the child who deems in sunshine that the stars have left the sky;
So by this world's pleasures dazzled, scarce we feel their presence true,—
In foolishness and fickleness are we not children too?

Seeing all my guilt and weakness, looking down with pitying eyes,
For the foolish things we cling to, and the Heaven that we despise,
They have been our guardian angels since this weary world began,
And they still are watching o'er for His sake who died for man!

FOR OF SUCH IS THE KINGDOM OF HEAVEN.

SWEET baby, sleep! what ails my dear,
    What ails my darling thus to cry?
  Be still, my child, and lend thine ear,
To hear me sing thy lullaby.
My pretty lamb, forbear to weep;
Be still, my dear; sweet baby, sleep.

Thou blessèd soul, what canst thou fear?
    What thing to thee can mischief do?
Thy God is now thy Father dear,
    His holy Spouse, thy mother too.
Sweet baby, then forbear to weep;
Be still, my babe; sweet baby, sleep.

While thus thy lullaby I sing,
    For thee great blessings ripening be;

Thine eldest brother is a king,
   And hath a kingdom bought for thee.
Sweet baby then forbear to weep;
Be still, my babe; sweet baby, sleep.

Sweet baby, sleep, and nothing fear;
   For whatsoever thee offends
By thy protector threatened are,
   And God and angels are thy friends.
Sweet baby, then forbear to weep;
Be still, my babe; sweet baby, sleep.

When God with us was dwelling here,
   In little babes He took delight;
Such innocents as thou, my dear,
   Are ever present in His sight.
Sweet baby, then forbear to weep;
Be still, my babe; sweet baby, sleep.

A little infant once was He;
   And strength in weakness then was laid
Upon His virgin mother's knee,
   That power to Thee might be conveyed.
Sweet baby, then forbear to weep;
Be still, my babe; sweet baby, sleep.

The wants that He did then sustain
  Have purchased wealth, my babe, for
    thee;
And by His torments and His pain
  Thy rest and ease securéd be.
My baby, then forbear to weep;
Be still, my babe; sweet baby, sleep.

Thou hast, yet more, to perfect this,
  A promise and an earnest got
Of gaining everlasting bliss,
  Though thou, my babe, perceivedst it not;
Sweet baby, then forbear to weep;
Be still, my babe; sweet baby, sleep.

     GEORGE WITHERS, (1641.)

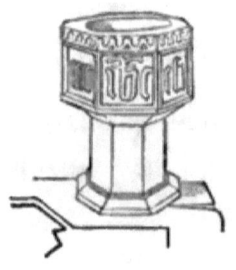

FOREVER WITH THE LORD.

LET me be with Thee where Thou art,
  My Saviour, my eternal Rest!
Then only will this longing heart
  Be fully and forever blest!

Let me be with Thee where Thou art,
  Where spotless saints Thy Name adore;
Then only will this sinful heart
  Be evil and defiled no more!

Let me be with Thee where Thou art,
  Where none can die, where none remove;
There neither death nor life will part
  Me from Thy Presence and Thy love!

        CHARLOTTE ELLIOTT, (1836.)

LIVE WHILE YOU LIVE.

'TIS not for man to trifle! Life is brief,
    And sin is here.
Our age is but the falling of a leaf—
    A dropping tear.
We have no time to sport away the hours;
All must be earnest in a world like ours.

Not many lives, but only one have we—
    Frail, fleeting man!
How sacred should that one life ever be—
    That narrow span!
Day after day filled up with blessed toil;
Hour after hour still bringing in new spoil!

Our being is no shadow of thin air,
    No vacant dream:
No fable of the things that never were,
    But only seem.
'Tis full of meaning as of mystery,
Though strange and solemn may that meaning be.

Our sorrows are no phantoms of the night—
    No idle tale:
No cloud that floats along a sky of light,
    On summer gale.
They are the true realities of earth—
Friends and companions even from our birth.

O, life below, how brief, how poor, how sad!
    One heavy sigh.
O, life above, how long, and fair, and glad!
    An endless joy.
Oh! to have done for aye with dying here!
Oh! to begin the living in yon sphere!

O, day of time, how dark! O, sky and earth,
    How dull your hue!
O, day of Christ, how bright! O, sky and earth,
    Made fair and new!
Come, better Eden, with thy fresher green!
Come, brighter Salem, gladden all the scene!

                        BONAR.

WE KNOW THAT WE HAVE PASSED FROM DEATH UNTO LIFE, BECAUSE WE LOVE THE BRETHREN.

THE clouds that wrap the setting sun
    When Autumn's softest gleams are ending,
    Where all bright hues together run
In sweet confusion blending:—
Why, as we watch their floating wreath,
Seem they the breath of life to breathe?
To Fancy's eye their motions prove
They mantle round the sun for love.

When up some woodland dell we catch
    The many-twinkling smile of ocean,
Or with pleased ear bewildered watch
    His chime of restless motion;
Still as the surging waves retire
They seem to grasp with strong desire,
Such signs of love old Ocean gives,
We cannot choose but think he lives.

Wouldst thou the life of souls discern?
  Nor human wisdom nor divine
Helps thee by aught beside to learn;
  Love is life's only sign.
The spring of the regenerate heart,
The pulse, the glow of every part,
Is the true love of Christ our Lord,
As man embraced, as God adored.

But he, whose heart will bound to mark
  The full bright bursts of summer morn,
Loves too each each little dewy spark
  By leaf or floweret worn:
Cheap forms, and common hues, 'tis true,
Through the bright shower-drop meet his view;
The colouring may be of this earth;
The lustre comes of heavenly birth.

Even so, who loves the Lord aright,
  No soul of man can worthless find;
All will be precious in his sight,
  Since Christ on all hath shined:
But chiefly Christian souls; for they,
Though worn and soiled with sinful clay,
Are yet, to eyes that see them rue,
All glistening with baptismal dew.

No distance breaks the tie of blood;
   Brothers are brothers evermore;
Nor wrong, nor wrath of deadliest mood,
     That magic may o'erpower;
Oft, ere the common source be known,
The kindred drops will claim their own,
And throbbing pulses silently
Move heart towards heart by sympathy.

So is it with true Christian hearts;
   Their mutual shares in Jesus' blood
An everlasting bond impart
     Of holiest brotherhood:
Oh! might we all our lineage prove,
Give and forgive, do good and love,
By soft endearments in kind strife
Lightening the load of daily life!

There is much need; for not as yet
   Are we in shelter or repose,
The holy house is still beset
     With leaguer of stern foes;
Wild thoughts within, bad men without,
All evil spirits round about,
Are banded in unblest device,
To spoil Love's earthly paradise.

Then draw we nearer day by day,
   Each to his brethren, all to God;

Let the world take us as she may,
    We must not change our road;
Not wondering, though in grief, to find
The martyr's foe still keep her mind;
But fixed to hold Love's banner fast,
And by submission win at last.
KEBLE.

REJOICE EVERMORE.

BUT how shall we be glad?
   We that are journeying through a vale
     of tears,
   Encompassed with a thousand woes
     and fears,
    How should not we be sad?

    Angels that ever stand
Within the presence chamber, and there raise
The never-interrupted hymn of praise,
    May welcome this command:

    Or they whose strife is o'er,
Who all their weary length of life hath trod,
As pillars now within the temple of God,
    That shall go out no more.

    But we who wander here,
We that are exiled in this gloomy place,
Still doomed to water Earth's unthankful face
    With many a bitter tear—

Bid us lament and mourn,
Bid us that we go mourning all the day,
And we will find it easy to obey,
    Of our best things forlorn:

But not that we be glad;
If it be true the mourners are the blest,
Oh, leave us in a world of sin, unrest,
    And trouble, to be sad!

I spoke and thought to weep—
For sin and sorrow, suffering and crime,
That fill the world, all mine appointed time
    A settled grief to keep.

When lo! as day from night,
As day from out the womb of night forlorn,
So from that sorrow was that gladness born,
    Even in mine own despite.

Yet was not that by this
Excluded—at the coming of that joy
Fled not that grief—nor did that grief destroy
    The newly-risen bliss:

But side by side they flow,
Two fountains flowing from one smitten heart
And ofttimes scarcely to be known apart—
    That gladness and that woe:

Two fountains from one source,
Or which from two such neighboring sources
    run,
That aye for him who shall unseal the one,
    The other flows perforce.

And both are sweet and calm,
Fair flowers upon the banks of either blow,
Both fertilize the soil, and where they flow
    Shed round them holy balm.

R. C. Trench.

SUNDAY.

DAY most calm, most bright!
The fruit of this, the next world's
   bud;
Th' endorsement of supreme delight,
Writ by a friend, and with his blood;
The couch of time; care's balm and bay,—
The week were dark, but for thy light;
   Thy torch doth shew the way.

Sundays the pillars are
On which heaven's palace arched lies:
The other days fill up the space
And hollow rooms with vanities.
They are the fruitful beds and borders,
In God's rich garden; that is bare,
   Which parts their ranks and orders.

The Sundays of man's life,
Threaded together on time's string,
Make bracelets to adorn the wife
Of the eternal, glorious King.

On Sunday, heaven's gate stands ope;
Blessings are plentiful and rife;
   More plentiful than hope.

Thou art a day of mirth:
And, where the week-days trail on ground,
Thy flight is higher, as thy birth.
O let me take thee at the bound,
Leaping with thee from seven to seven;
Till that we both, being tossed from earth,
   Fly hand in hand to heaven.
GEORGE HERBERT.

THE LORD'S DAY.

TIME of tranquil joy and holy feel-
   ing!
When over earth God's spirit from
   above
   Spreads out His wings of love!
When sacred thoughts, like angels, come appeal-
   ing
To our tent doors; O loeve; to earth and heaven
   The sweetest of the seven!

How peaceful are thy skies! thy air is clearer,
As on the advent of a gracious time:
   The sweetness of its prime
Blesseth the world, and Eden's days seem
   nearer:
I hear, in each faint stirring of the breeze,
   God's voice among the trees.

O while thy hallowed moments are distilling
Their fresher influence on my heart like dews,
   The chamber when I muse

Turns to a temple! He, whose converse thrill-
    ing
Honored Emmaüs, that old eventide,
    Comes sudden to my side.

'Tis light at evening time when Thou art pres
    ent;
Thy coming to the eleven in that dim room
    Brightened, O Christ! its gloom:
So bless my lonely hour that memories pleasant
Around the time a heavenly gleam may cast,
    Which many days shall last!

Raise each low aim, refine each high emotion,
That with more ardent footstep I may press
    Toward Thy holiness;
And, braced for sacred duty by devotion,
Support my cross along that rugged road
    Which Thou hast sometimes trod!

I long to see Thee, for my heart is weary:
O when, my Lord! in kindness wilt Thou
    come
    To call Thy banished home?
The scenes are cheerless, and the days are
    dreary;
From sorrow and from sin I would be free,
    And evermore with Thee!

Even now I see the golden city shining
Up the blue depths of that transparent air:
    How happy all is there!
There breaks a day which never knows declining;
A Sabbath, through whose circling hours the blest
    Beneath Thy shadow rest!
JAMES D. BURNS, (1855.)

EARLY RISING AND PRAYER.

WHEN first thy eyes unveil, give thy soul leave
To do the like; our bodies but forerun
The spirit's duty: true hearts spread and heave
Unto their God, as flowers do to the sun:
Give Him thy first thoughts then, so shalt thou keep
Him company all day, and in Him sleep.

Yet never sleep the sun up; prayer should
Dawn with the day: there are set awful hours
'Twixt heaven and us; the manna was not good
After sun-rising; for day sullies flowers:
Rise to prevent the sun; sleep doth sins glut,
And heaven's gate opens when the world's is shut.

Walk with thy fellow creatures; note the hush
And whispering amongst them. Not a spring
Or leaf but hath his morning hymn; each bush
And oak doth know I AM. Canst thou not sing!
O leave thy cares and follies! Go this way,
And thou art sure to prosper all the day.

Serve God before the world; let him not go
Until thou hast a blessing; then resign
The whole unto him and remember who
Prevail'd by wrestling ere the sun did shine;
Pour oil upon the stones, weep for thy sin,
Then journey on and have an eye to heaven.

Mornings are mysteries; the first, the world's youth,
Man's resurrection, and the future's bud,
Shroud in their births; the crown of life, light, truth
Is styl'd their star; the stone and hidden food:
Three blessings wait upon them, one of which
Should move, — they make us holy, happy, rich.

When the world's up, and every swarm abroad,
Keep well thy temper, mix not with each clay;

Despatch necessities; life hath a load
Which must be carried on, and safely may;
Yet keep those cares without thee; let the heart
Be God's alone, and choose the better part.
    HENRY C. VAUGHN, (1614.)

MORNING.

 TIMELY happy, timely wise,
Hearts that with rising morn arise!
Eyes that the beam celestial view,
Which evermore makes all things new!

New every morning is the love
Our wakening and uprising prove,
Through sleep and darkness safely brought,
Restored to life, and power, and thought.

New mercies, each returning day,
Hover around us while we pray;
New perils past, new sins forgiven,
New thoughts of God, new hopes of Heaven.

If, on our daily course, our mind
Be set to hallow all we find,
New treasures still, of countless price,
God will provide the sacrifice.

Old friends, old scenes, will lovelier be,
As more of Heaven in each we see;
Some softening gleam of love and prayer
Shall dawn on every cross and care.

As for some dear familiar strain
Untired we ask, and ask again;
Ever, in its melodious store,
Finding a spell unheard before;

Such is the bliss of souls serene,
When they have sworn, and steadfast mean,
Counting the cost, in all t'espy
Their God, in all themselves deny.

O could we learn that sacrifice,
What lights would all around us rise!
How would our hearts with wisdom talk
Along life's dullest, dreariest walk!

We need not bid, for cloistered cell,
Our neighbour and our work farewell,
Nor strive to wind ourselves too high
For sinful man beneath the sky:

The trivial round, the common task,
Will furnish all we ought to ask;

Room to deny ourselves; a road
To bring us, daily, nearer God.

Seek we no more: content with these,
Let present rapture, comfort, ease,
As Heaven shall bid them, come and go;
The secret this, of rest below.

Only, O Lord, in Thy dear love
Fit us for perfect rest above;
And help us, this day and every day,
To live more nearly as we pray.

JOHN KEBLE, (1827.)

AS THY DAY IS.

SINCE Thou hast added now, O God!
  Unto my life another day,
  And giv'st me leave to walk abroad,
  And labour in my lawful way;
My walks and works with me begin,
Conduct me forth, and bring me in.

In every power my soul enjoys
  Internal virtues to improve;
In every sense that she employs
  In her external works to move;
Bless her, O God! and keep me sound
From outward harm and inward wound.

Let sin nor Satan's fraud prevail
  To make mine eye of reason blind,
Or faith, or hope, or love to fail,
  Or any virtues of the mind;
But more and more let them increase,
And bring me to mine end in peace.

Lewd courses let my feet forbear;
   Keep Thou my hands from doing wrong;
Let not ill counsels pierce mine ear,
   Nor wicked words defile my tongue;
And keep the windows of each eye
That no strange lust climb in thereby.

But guard Thou safe my heart in chief;
   That neither hate, revenge, nor fear,
Nor vain desire, vain joy or grief,
   Obtain command or dwelling there:
And, Lord! with every saving grace,
Still true to Thee maintain that place!

So till the evening of this morn
   My time shall then so well be spent,
That when the twilight shall return
   I may enjoy it with content,
And to Thy praise and honour say,
That this hath proved a happy day.
            GEORGE WITHERS, (1641).

ABIDE WITH US.

ABIDE with me; fast falls the eventide;
The darkness; Lord, with me abide:
When other keepers fail, and comforts flee,
Help of the helpless; O abide with me.

Swift to the close ebbs out life's little day;
Earth's joys grow dim, its glories pass away;
Changes and decay in all around I see;
O Thou who changest not, abide with me!

I need Thy presence every passing hour;
What but Thy grace can foil the tempter's power?
Who, like Thyself, my guide and stay can be?
Through cloud and sunshine, Lord, abide with me!

I fear no foe: with Thee at hand to bless,
Ills have no weight, and tears no bitterness;
Where is death's sting? where, grave, thy victory?
I triumph still, if Thou abide with me.

Hold Thou Thy cross before my closing eyes;
Shine through the gloom, and point me to the skies;—
Heaven's morning breaks, and earth's vain shadows flee,—
In life, in death, O Lord, abide with me!

LYTE.

EVENING.

SUN of my soul, Thou Saviour dear,
It is not night if Thou be near;
Oh! may no earth-born cloud arise
To hide Thee from Thy servant's eyes!

When round Thy wondrous works below
My searching rapturous glance I throw,
Tracing out wisdom, power, and love,
In earth or sky, in stream or grove;

Or, by the light Thy words disclose,
Watch time's full river as it flows,
Scanning Thy gracious Providence,
Where not too deep for mortal sense;

When with dear friends sweet talk I hold,
And all the flowers of life unfold;
Let not my heart within me burn,
Except in all I Thee discern!

When the soft dews of kindly sleep
My wearied eyelids gently steep,
Be my last thoughts, how sweet to rest
For ever on my Saviour's breast!

Abide with me from morn till eve,
For without Thee I cannot live!
Abide with me when night is nigh,
For without Thee I dare not die!

Thou framer of the light and dark,
Steer through the tempest Thine own ark!
Amid the howling mighty sea
We are in port if we have Thee.

The rulers of this Christian land,
Twixt Thee and us ordained to stand,
Guide Thou their course, O Lord, aright!
Let all do all as in Thy sight!

Oh! by Thine own sad burthen, borne
So meekly up the hill of scorn,
Teach Thou Thy priests their daily cross,
To bear as Thine, nor count it loss!

If some poor wandering child of Thine
Have spurned to-day the voice divine;

Now, Lord, the gracious work begin ;
Let him no more lie down in sin !

Watch by the sick—enrich the poor
With blessings from Thy boundless store !
Be every mourner's sleep to-night
Like infant's slumber, pure and light !

Come near and bless us when we wake,
Ere through the world our way we take ;
Till, in the ocean of Thy love,
We lose ourselves in Heaven above !

JOHN KEBLE, (1827.)

DAY BY DAY WE MAGNIFY THEE.

STAR of morn and even,
  Sun of Heaven's heaven,
    Saviour high and dear,
    Toward us turn Thine ear;
  Through whate'er may come,
  Thou canst lead us home.

Though the gloom be grievous,
Those we leant on leave us,
    Though the coward heart,
    Quit its proper part,
  Though the tempter come,
  Thou wilt lead us home.

Saviour pure and holy,
Lover of the lowly,
    Sign us with Thy sign,
    Take our hands in Thine,
  Take our hands and come,
  Lead Thy children home!

Star of morn and even,
Shine on us from Heaven,
From Thy glory-throne
Hear Thy very own!
Lord and Saviour come,
Lead us to our home!

FRANCIS TURNER PALGROVE, (1862.)

I AM WITH YOU ALWAYS.

NOT Thou from us, O Lord, but we
Withdraw ourselves from Thee.
When we are dark and dead
And Thou art covered with a cloud,
Hanging before Thee, like a shroud,
So that our prayers can find no way,
Oh! teach us that we do not say,
"Where is *Thy* brightness fled?"

But that we search and try
What in ourselves has wrought this blame;
For Thou remainest still the same,
But earth's own vapours earth may fill
With darkness and thick clouds, while still
The sun is in the sky.

R. C. Trench.

I WILL ARISE AND GO TO MY FATHER.

Just as I am—without one plea,
But that Thy blood was shed for me,
And that Thou bid'st me come to Thee—
   O Lamb of God, I come.

Just as I am—and waiting not
To rid my soul of one dark blot,
To Thee, Whose blood can cleanse each spot—
   O Lamb of God, I come.

Just as I am—though tossed about
With many a conflict, many a doubt,
With fears within and foes without—
   O Lamb of God, I come.

Just as I am—poor, weary, blind;
Sight, riches, healing of the mind,
Yea, all I need, in Thee I find—
   O Lamb of God, I come.

Just as I am—Thou wilt receive,
Wilt welcome, pardon, cleanse, relieve,
Because Thy promise I believe—
    O Lamb of God, I come.

Just as I am—Thy love, unknown,
Has broken every barrier down;
Now to be Thine, yea, Thine alone—
    O Lamb of God, I come.
CHARLOTTE ELLIOTT.

THIS DID NOT ONCE SO TROUBLE ME.

This did not once so trouble me,
    That better I could not love Thee,
      But now I feel and know
    That only when we love, we find
How far our hearts remain behind
    The love they should bestow.

While we had little care to call
On Thee, and scarcely prayed at all,
    We seemed enough to pray:
But now we only think with shame,
How seldom to Thy glorious Name
    Our lips their offerings pay.

And when we gave yet slighter heed
Unto our brother's suffering need,
    Our hearts reproached us then
Not half so much as now, that we
With such a careless eye can see
    The woes and wants of men.

In doing this is knowledge won,
To see what yet remains undone;
  With this our pride repress,
And give us grace a growing store,
That day by day we may do more,
  And may esteem it less.

R. C. Trench.

A WALK IN A CHURCHYARD.

WE walked within the churchyard bounds,
  My little boy and I—
He laughing, running happy rounds,
  I pacing mournfully.

"Nay, child! it is not well," I said,
  "Among the graves to shout,
To laugh and play among the dead,
  And make this noisy rout."

A moment to my side he clung,
  Leaving his merry play,
A moment stilled his joyous tongue,
  Almost as hushed as they:

Then quite forgetting the command
  In life's exulting burst
Of early glee, let go my hand,
  Joyous as at the first.

And now I did not check him more,
  For, taught by Nature's face,
I had grown wiser than before
  Even in that moment's space.

She spread no funeral-pall above
  That patch of churchyard ground,
But the same azure vault of love
  As hung o'er all around.

And white clouds o'er that spot would pass,
  As freely as elsewhere;
The sunshine on no other grass
  A richer hue might wear.

And formed from out that very mould
  In which the dead did lie,
The daisy with its eye of gold
  Looked up into the sky.

The rook was wheeling overhead,
  Nor hastening to be gone—
The small bird did its glad notes shed,
  Perched on a gray head-stone.

And God, I said, would never give
  This light upon the earth,
Nor bid in childhood's heart to live
  These springs of gushing mirth—

If our one wisdom were to mourn,
    And linger with the dead,
To nurse, as wisest, thoughts forlorn
    Of worm and earthy bed.

Oh, no! the glory earth puts on,
    The child's unchecked delight,
Both witness to a triumph won,
    (If we did but read aright)—

A triumph won o'er sin and death,
    From these the Saviour saves;
And like a happy infant, Faith
    Can play among the graves.

R. C. Trench.

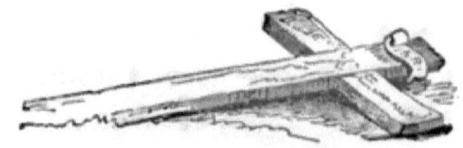

THE WANDERER.

FAR from the Shepherd's one true fold
    I stray,
  In pathways all unknown;
   O dark and gloomy is the woeful day
That finds me here alone.

My hopes are blighted, and my heart bereft
    Of comfort and repose,
Because the Shepherd's blessed Fold I left,
    To wander where I chose.

I sought more liberty and less restraint;
    My will I wished to please;
And all day long I made a vain complaint,
    In greater rest and ease.

At last I broke away and left the flock,
    To find a desert bare—
No food, no cooling stream, no sheltering rock,—
    False dreams and blank despair.

O for the Fold, the blessed Fold once more!
    O for the Shepherd's hand,
To guide me back, and lead me as of yore
    In verdant pasture land!

O seek me, tender Shepherd, lest I die;
    Find me and take me home;
Once there again in calm security,
    My feet shall never roam.

Thy staff may strike—I will not shrink again,
    Or spurn Thy warning voice,
Or seek a pathway without toil or pain,
    Of mine own erring choice.

But in the footsteps of the flock, Thy way
    With duteous love I'll take,
And strive to curb my will, and day by day
    All devious ways forsake.

Then seek me tender Shepherd, lest I die,
    Or further from Thee roam;
In pity heed Thy wanderer's heart-wrung cry,
    And bring me safely home.

E. L. LEE.

UNTO THE PERFECT DAY.

OUR course is onward, onward into light:
What though the darkness gathereth amain,
Yet to return or tarry, both are vain.
How tarry, when around is thick night?
Whither return? what flower yet ever might,
In days of gloom, and cold, and stormy rain,
Enclose itself in its green bud again,
Hiding from wrath of tempest out of sight?
Courage!—we travel through a darksome cave;
But still as nearer to the light we draw,
Fresh gales will reach us from the upper air,
And wholesome dews of heaven our foreheads lave,
The darkness lighten more, till full of awe
We stand in the open sunshine—unaware.

R. C. TRENCH.

VIRTUE.

SWEET Day! so cool, so calm, so bright;
The bridal of the earth and sky:
The dew shall weep thy fall to-night;
For thou must die.

Sweet Rose! whose hue, angry and brave,
Bids the rash gazer wipe his eye:
Thy root is ever in its grave:—
And thou must die.

Sweet Spring! full of sweet days and roses;
A box where sweets compacted lie;
My music shews you have your closes:—
And all must die.

Only a sweet and virtuous soul,
Like seasoned timber, never gives;
But, though the whole world turn to coal,
    Then chiefly lives.

            GEORGE HERBERT.

DEATH'S FINAL CONQUEST.

THE glories of our birth and state,
    Are shadows not substantial things;
There is no armour against fate:
    Death lays his icy hands on kings;
        Sceptre and crown
        Must tumble down,
And in the dust be equal made
With the poor crooked scythe and spade.

Some men with swords may reap the field,
    And plant fresh laurels where they kill;
But their strong nerves at last must yield,
    They tame but one another still;
        Early or late,
        They stoop to fate,
And must give up their murmuring breath,
When they, pale captives, creep to death.

The garlands wither on your brow,
    Then boast no more your mighty deeds;

Upon Death's purple altar, now,
  See where the victor victim bleeds:
      All heads must come
      To the cold tomb,
Only the actions of the just
Smell sweet and blossom in the dust.
            JAMES SHIRLEY, (1646.)

MY LIFE DRAWETH NIGH TO THE GRAVE.

SO rest, my Rest,
    For ever blest,
  Thy grave with sinners making
  By Thy precious death from sin
    My dead soul awaking.

  Here hast Thou lain,
    After much pain,
Life of my life, reposing:
Round Thee now a rock-hewn grave,
    Rock of ages closing.

  Breath of all breath,
    I know, from death
Thou wilt my dust awaken;
Wherefore should I dread the grave,
    Or my faith be shaken?

To me the tomb
  Is but a room
Where I lie down on roses;
Who by death hath conquered death,
  Sweetly there reposes.

The body dies
  (Nought else) and lies
In dust, until victorious
From the grave it shall arise
  Beautiful and glorious.

Meantime I will,
  My Jesus still
Deep in my bosom lay Thee,
Musing on Thy death: in death
  Be with me, I pray Thee.

THE JERUSALEM THAT IS ABOVE.

I.

BRIEF life is here our portion;
    Brief sorrow, short-lived care;
The life that knows no ending,
    The tearless life, is *there*.

O happy retribution
    Short toil, eternal rest :
For mortals and for sinners
    A mansion with the blest.

And now we fight the battle,
    But then shall wear the crown
Of full and everlasting
    And passionless renown :

And now we watch and struggle,
    And now we live in hope,

And Sion in her anguish
  With Babylon must cope:

But He whom now we trust in
  Shall then be seen and known;
And they that know and see Him
  Shall have Him for their own.

The morning shall awaken,
  The shadows flee away,
And each true-hearted servant
  Shall shine as doth the day.

There God, our King and Patron,
  In fulness of His grace,
Shall we behold forever
  And worship face to face.

II.

For thee, O dear, dear country,
  Mine eyes their vigils keep;
For very love beholding
  Thy happy name, they weep.

The mention of Thy glory
  Is unction to the breast,
And medicine in sickness,
  And love, and light, and rest.

O one, O only Mansion!
    O Paradise of Joy!
Where tears are ever banished,
    And smiles have no alloy:

The Lamb is all thy splendour,
    The Crucified thy praise;
His land and benediction
    Thy ransomed people praise.

With jasper glow thy bulwarks,
    Thy streets with emeralds blaze;
The sardius and the topaz
    Unite in thee their rays;

Thine ageless walls are bonded
    With amethyst unpriced;
The saints build up the fabric,
    And the corner-stone is Christ.

Thou hast no shore, fair ocean!
    Thou hast no time, bright day!
Dear fountain of refreshment
    To pilgrims far away!

Upon the Rock of Ages
    They raise thy holy tower;
Thine is the victor's laurels,
    And thine the golden dower.

III.

Jerusalem the golden!
  With milk and honey blest!
Beneath thy contemplation
  Sink heart and voice opprest.

I know not, oh! I know not
  What joys await us there;
What radiancy of glory,
  What bliss beyond compare.

They stand, those halls of Sion,
  All jubilant with song,
And bright with many an Angel,
  And all the martyr throng:

The Prince is ever in them,
  The daylight ever bright;
The pastures of the blessed
  Are decked in glorious light.

There is the throne of David;
  And there from care released,
The shout of them that triumph,
  The song of them that feast;

And they, who with their Leader
  Have conquered in the fight,

Forever and forever
  And clad in robes of white.

O sweet and blessed country,
  The home of God's elect!
O sweet and blessed country,
  That eager hearts expect!

Jesu, in mercy bring us
  To that dear land of rest:
Who art, with God the Father,
  And Spirit, ever blest.   Amen.

From St. Bernard.

LIFE.

I MADE a posy, while the day ran by;
"Here will I smell my remnant out, and tie
My life within this band."
But Time did beckon to the flowers, and they
By noon most cunningly did steal away,
And wither in my hand.

My hand was next to them, and then my heart.
I took, without more thinking, in good part
Time's gentle admonition;
Who did so sweetly death's sad task convey,
Making my mind to smell my fatal day,
Yet sugaring my suspicion.

Farewell dear flowers! sweetly your time ye spent;
Fit, while ye liv'd, for smell or ornament;

And, after death, for cures.
I follow straight, without complaint or grief;
Since, if my scent be good, I care not if
    It be short as yours.
        GEORGE HERBERT, (1620.)

SEEKING A COUNTRY.

NOT here! not here! not where the sparkling waters
  Fade into mocking sands as we draw near,
Where in the wilderness each footstep falters—
  " I shall be satisfied!"—but oh, not here!

Not here—where all the dreams of bliss deceive us,
  Where the worn spirit never gains its goal;
Where, haunted ever by the thoughts that grieve us,
  Across us floods of bitter memory roll.

There is a land where every pulse is thrilling
  With rapture earth's sojourners may not know,
Where Heaven's repose the weary heart is stilling,
  And peacefully life's time-tossed currents flow.

Far out of sight, while sorrows still enfold us,
  Lies the fair Country where our hearts abide,

And of its bliss is nought more wondrous told us,
　Than these few words, "I shall be satisfied."

"I shall be satisfied!" The spirit's yearning
　For sweet companionship with kindred minds—
The silent love that here meets no returning—
　The inspiration which no language finds—

Shall they be satisfied? The soul's vague longing—
　The aching void which nothing earthly fills?
O! what desires upon my heart are thronging,
　As I look upward to the heavenly hills!

Thither my weak and weary steps are tending—
　Saviour and Lord! with Thy frail child abide!
Guide me toward Home, where, all my wanderings ending,
　I shall see Thee, and "shall be satisfied."

MY SHEEP HEAR MY VOICE.

HARK! hark! my soul! angelic songs are swelling
    O'er earth's green fields and ocean's wave-beat shore!
How sweet the truth those blessed strains are telling
    Of that new life when sin shall be no more!

Darker than night, life's shadows fall around us,
    And, like benighted men, we miss our mark;
God hides Himself, and grace hath scarcely found us,
    Ere death finds out his victims in the dark!

Onward we go, for still we hear them singing,
    Come weary souls! for Jesus bids you come!
And through the dark its echoes, sweetly ringing,
    The music of the Gospel leads us home.

Far, far away, like bells at evening pealing,
    The voice of Jesus sounds o'er land and sea,

And laden souls, by myriads meekly stealing,
  Kind Shepherd, turn their weary steps to Thee.

Rest comes at length; though life be long and dreary,
  The day must dawn and darksome night be past;
All journeys end in welcomes to the weary,
  And heaven, the heart's true home, will come at last.

Cheer up my soul! faith's moonbeams softly glisten
  Upon the breast of life's most troubled sea;
And it will cheer thy drooping heart to listen
  To those brave songs which angels mean for thee.

Angels! sing on, your faithful watches keeping,
  Sing us sweet fragments of the songs above;
While we toil on, and soothe ourselves with weeping,
  Till life's long night shall break in endless love.

Oratory Hymns.

THE DEATH OF A CHRISTIAN.

THE Apostle slept,—a light shone in the prison,
    An angel touched his side;
"Arise!" he said; and quickly he hath risen,
    His fettered arms untied.

The watchers saw no light at midnight gleaming,
    They heard no sound of feet;
The gates fly open, and the saint, still dreaming,
    Stands free upon the street.

So when the Christian's eyelid droops and closes
    In nature's parting strife,
A friendly Angel stands where he reposes,
    To wake him up to life.

He gives a gentle blow, and so releases
    The spirit from its clay;
From sin's temptations, and from life's distresses,
    He bids it come away.

It rises up, and from its darksome mansion
    It takes its silent flight;
And feels its freedom in the large expansion
    Of heavenly air and light.

Behind, it hears Time's iron gates close faintly,
    It now is far from them;
For it has reached the City of the saintly,
    The New Jerusalem.

A voice is heard on earth of kinsfolk weeping
    The loss of one they love:
But he is gone where the redeemed are keeping
    A Festival above!

The mourners throng the way, and from the steeple
    The funeral-bell tolls slow;
But on the golden streets the holy people
    Are passing to and fro;

And singing as they meet, "Rejoice! another,
    Long waited for, is come;"
The Saviour's heart is glad, a younger brother
    Hath reached the Father's Home!
J. D. BURNS.

THE VANITY OF THE WORLD.

FALSE world, thou ly'st: thou canst
    not lend
      The least delight:
    Thy favours cannot gain a friend,
      They are so slight:
Thy morning's pleasures make an end
      To please at night:
Poor are the wants that thou supply'st,
And yet thou vaun'st, and yet thou vy'st
With heaven; fond earth, thou boasts; false
      world, thou ly'st.

Thy babbling tells of golden tales
      Of endless treasure;
Thy bounty offers easy sales
      Of lasting pleasure;
Thou ask'st the conscience what she ails,
      And swear'st to ease her:
There's none can want where thou sup-
      ply'st:

There's none can give where thou deny'st.
Alas! fond world, thou boasts; false world,
    thou ly'st.

What well-advisèd ear regards
    What earth can say?
Thy words are gold, but thy rewards
    Are painted clay:
Thy cunning can but pack the cards,
    Thou canst not play:
Thy game at weakest, still thou vy'st;
If seen, and then revy'd, deny'st:
Thou art not what thou seem'st; false world,
    thou ly'st.

Thy timid bosom seems a mint
    Of new-coin'd treasure;
A paradise, that has no stint,
    No change, no measure;
A painted cask, but nothing in't,
    Nor wealth, nor pleasure:
Vain earth! that falsely thus comply'st
With man; vain man! that thou rely'st
On earth, vain man, thou dot'st; vain earth,
    thou ly'st.

What mean dull souls, in this high measure,
    To haberdash

To earth's base wares, whose greatest treasure
        Is dross and trash?
The height of whose enchanting pleasure
        Is but a flash?
Are these the goods that thou supply'st
Us mortals with? are these the high'st?
Can these bring cordial peace? false world, thou
        ly'st.

F. Quarles.

ALL THE ANGELS STOOD ABOUT THE THRONE.

THERE is no night in heaven:
    In that blest world above
  Work never can bring weariness,
    For work itself is love.
  There is no night in heaven:
    Yet nightly round the bed
Of every Christian wanderer
    Faith has an angel tread.

  There is no grief in heaven:
    For life is one glad day,
And tears are of those former things
    Which all have passed away.
  There is no grief in heaven:
    Yet angels from on high
On golden pinions earthward glide,
    The Christian's tears to dry.

There is no want in heaven:
  The Lamb of God supplies
Life's tree of twelvefold fruitage still,
  Life's spring which never dries.
There is no want in heaven:
  Yet in a desert land
The fainting prophet was sustained
  And fed by angel's hand.

There is no sin in heaven:
  Behold that blessèd throng;
All holy is their spotless robe,
  All holy is their song.
There is no sin in heaven:
  Here who from sin is free?
Yet angels aid us in our strife
  For Christ's true liberty.

There is no death in heaven:
  For they who gain that shore
Have won their immortality,
  And they can die no more.
There is no death in heaven:
  But, when the Christian dies,
The angels wait his parting soul,
  And waft it to the skies.

THE LAMB IS THE LIGHT THEREOF.

WHAT clime is not like this dull clime
    of ours;
  All, all is brightness there;
  A sweeter influence breathes around
    its flowers,
  And a benigner air.
No calm below is like that calm above,
No region here is like that realm of love;
Earth's softest spring ne'er shed so soft a light,
Earth's brightest summer never shone so bright.

That sky is not like this sad sky of ours,
  Tinged with earth's change and care:
No shadow dims it, and no rain-cloud lowers:
  No broken sunshine there:
One everlasting stretch of azure pours
Its stainless splendour o'er those sinless shores:
For there Jehovah shines with heavenly ray,
And Jesus reigns dispensing endless day.

The dwellers there are not like those of earth;
    No mortal stain they bear;
And yet they seem of kindred blood and birth;
    Whence and how came they there?
Earth was their native soil; from sin and shame,
Through tribulation, they to glory came;
Bond-slaves delivered from sin's crushing load,
Brands plucked from burning by the hand of
    God.

Yon robes of theirs are not like those below;
    No angel's half so bright:
Whence came that beauty, whence that living
    glow,
    And whence that radiant white?
Washed in the blood of the atoning Lamb,
Fair as the light these robes of theirs became;
And now, all tears wiped off from every eye,
They wander where the freshest pastures lie,
Through all the nightless day of that unfading
    sky.

www.ingramcontent.com/pod-product-compliance
Lightning Source LLC
Chambersburg PA
CBHW030818230426
43667CB00008B/1266